Antidiscrimination Law and Minority Employment

Farrell Bloch

Antidiscrimination Law and Minority Employment

RECRUITMENT PRACTICES AND REGULATORY CONSTRAINTS

The University of Chicago Press • Chicago and London

FARRELL BLOCH is an economic and statistical consultant in Washington, D.C. He is the author of *Statistics for Nonstatisticians* and editor of *Evaluating Manpower Training Programs.*

The University of Chicago Press, Chicago 60637
The University of Chicago Press, Ltd., London
© 1994 by The University of Chicago
All rights reserved. Published 1994
Printed in the United States of America
03 02 01 00 99 98 97 96 95 94   1 2 3 4 5
ISBN: 0-226-05983-9 (cloth)

Library of Congress Cataloging-in-Publication Data

Bloch, Farrell E.
    Antidiscrimination law and minority employment : recruitment
practices and regulatory constraints / Farrell Bloch.
        p.   cm.
    Includes bibliographical references and index.
    1. Discrimination in employment—Law and legislation—United
States.   2. Minorities—Employment—United States.   3. Employees—
Recruiting—Law and legislation—United States.   I. Title.
KF3464.B54   1994
344.73'01133—dc20
[347.3041133]   93-44408
                                                              CIP

To Gertrude Bloch, my mother
and
to the memory of Jules Bloch, my father

CONTENTS

List of Tables ix

Acknowledgments x

1   INTRODUCTION   1

2   RECRUITMENT PRACTICES   6

    2.1 Word-of-Mouth Recruitment   9

    2.2 Other Recruitment Practices   13

    2.3 Alternatives to In-House Recruitment   17

    2.4 Initial Applicant Evaluation   20

    2.5 The Use and Efficacy of Job-Seeking Methods   25

3   RECRUITMENT DISCRIMINATION   28

    3.1 Hiring Discrimination   29

    3.2 Recruitment Discrimination   36

    3.3 Applicant Screening   45

4   EMPLOYMENT DISCRIMINATION LAW   48

    4.1 Employment Discrimination Law in the United States   48

    4.2 Disparate Impact Recruitment Allegations   53

    4.3 Affirmative Action   70

5   ANTIDISCRIMINATION POLICY:
THEORETICAL CONSIDERATIONS   74

    5.1 Basic Principles   74

    5.2 The Discrimination Paradigm   79

    5.3 Efficiency   81

    5.4 Equity   85

    5.5 Administrative Costs   86

6   THE EFFECTS OF ANTIDISCRIMINATION PROGRAMS   88
     6.1 Effects of Title VII of the Civil Rights Act of 1964   89
     6.2 Effects of the Federal Contract Compliance Program   96
     6.3 Interpretation   99
     6.4 Private Policy   109
     6.5 Public Policy   111

7   MINORITY EMPLOYMENT OPPORTUNITIES   117
     7.1 Conventional Employment Policies   117
     7.2 Inner-City Unemployment   122
     7.3 Recruitment and Certification   127

     Author Index   133

     Subject Index   136

TABLES

3.1	Entrepreneurship and Unemployment	39
3.2	Unemployment Rates by Race: Age Sixteen and Over	41
3.3	Unemployment Rates by Race: Age Twenty and Over	42
5.1	Employees in Contractor and EEO-1 Reporting Firms	84
6.1	Budget and Staffing of the Equal Employment Opportunity Commission	92
6.2	Budget and Staffing of the Office of Federal Contract Compliance Programs	97
6.3	Distribution of Work Force by Size of Establishment	100
6.4	Representation of Minorities and Women	102

ACKNOWLEDGMENTS

For help with this book, I am grateful to many. My clients and their attorneys afforded me an insight into the operation of labor markets that complements my academic training. Open door policies of university and government libraries allowed easy access to research materials. Federal officials at the Bureau of the Census, the Department of Labor, and the Equal Employment Opportunity Commission kindly provided data, much of it unpublished. And the editors and readers at the University of Chicago Press gave helpful advice as they shepherded my manuscript into book form.

My greatest debt is to three friends who read my initial draft and provided valuable suggestions. Burt Barnow's detailed written comments addressed even peripheral statements in footnotes. Tony Pellechio added the perspective of an applied economist encountering other forms of regulation. And Marc Rosenblum taught me much about employment discrimination law, and brought to my attention relevant articles in the legal literature. Neither they nor those indirectly acknowledged here necessarily concur with my conclusions, nor are they responsible for any errors that might remain.

CHAPTER ONE

Introduction

Despite almost thirty years of antidiscrimination and affirmative action regulation in the United States, the unemployment rate of blacks has remained twice that of whites. Why hasn't this gap narrowed?

This book suggests four reasons. First, federal policies appear to have redistributed black workers from small and medium-sized firms to large employers and federal contractors—without improving their aggregate employment. Heavily regulated companies apparently recruit minority employees who would otherwise be available to smaller firms. Second, to reduce their exposure to litigation, employers have incentives to avoid hiring minority, female, and older workers. Employees are far more likely than applicants to file discrimination lawsuits, and damages awarded to them tend to be greater than those received by applicants. Third, the laws generally cannot benefit those who do not discover job opportunities made known only through word-of-mouth networks. Because blacks, Hispanics, and American Indians have relatively low rates of entrepreneurship, their job recruitment networks are not as fruitful as those of whites and Asian-Americans. Indeed, entrepreneurship and unemployment rates are strongly negatively correlated across demographic groups. Fourth, in deciding which applicants will become serious job candidates, employers favor initial screening criteria that disproportionately exclude minorities.

In short, employer recruitment practices, some of which are reactive to federal policy, severely limit the impact of government regulation. Empirically, with the exception of the 1964 Civil Rights Act's repeal of southern segregation, the nexus of antidiscrimination and affirmative action law appears not to have benefited blacks *as an aggregate,* although it is conceivable that future research will demonstrate a substantial impact that has been offset by such phenomena as the loss of manufacturing jobs, demand shifts favoring skilled

1

over unskilled labor, growing suburbanization of employment, and increasing drug traffic and crime that discourage business formation in inner cities.

Because economists have given relatively little attention to the processes by which employers generate job applicants, I devote chapter 2 to recruitment practices before beginning any discussion of discrimination. The remaining chapters emphasize recruitment's impact on minority job seekers without analyzing in detail other employer policies. Certainly hiring criteria such as tests—as well as termination practices—affect employment. Moreover, the antidiscrimination laws address pay, promotion, and other aspects of employment as well as hiring. Nonetheless, recruitment itself explains a great deal. And in addition to investigating the powerful yet little analyzed effects on minority employment of the methods companies enlist to attract applicants, a secondary objective of this book is to present a general discussion of employee recruitment in the hope of motivating research in this neglected area.

Chapter 2 gives particular attention to word-of-mouth recruitment, the means by which many job seekers, particularly lower-skilled workers in small establishments, find jobs. I propose that relative to their fellow employees, those recruited via word-of-mouth networks will earn more, enjoy rapid initial pay and productivity increases, and quit and be fired less often. Like effects obtain for those working with friends or culturally similar coworkers. Lower pay rates are expected for those commuting with neighbors or friends, whether coworkers or not.

In addition to capitalizing on word-of-mouth networks, employers place classified ads, accept direct applications from walk-ins, seek referrals from employment agencies, and rely on targeted recruitment methods—such as placing help-wanted ads in foreign language newspapers—by which members of certain ethnic groups are more likely than others to be informed of job vacancies. Alternatives to recruitment include assigning overtime to current employees, and retaining temporary help agencies and firms providing business services.

Although hiring practices are not the focus of this book, chapter 2 includes a section on *initial* applicant evaluation. Because it is costly to interview and otherwise to evaluate applicants, employers reject some job seekers on the basis of information on their application forms and résumés. Chapter 3 demonstrates how these criteria adversely affect minority applicants. For example, if suburban employers believe that employees living near their jobs will be more punctual, they will summarily reject applicants living far away—thereby disproportionately excluding blacks, Hispanics, and others concentrated in cities.

Minority job seekers also face direct hiring and recruitment discrimination. Many employers believe that minorities, particularly urban blacks, generally will be less productive than other workers, and they find it too costly to determine when individual applicants do not conform to these stereotypes. A disinclination to hire minorities translates into failure to recruit them. Furthermore, many recruitment policies have serious implications for minority job seekers, whether intended or not. As in the example of the previous paragraph, suburban employers concerned about hiring those living far away may place help-wanted ads only in suburban newspapers rather than in major metropolitan dailies, thereby reaching few minorities. And because social networks are somewhat ethnically stratified, word-of-mouth recruitment tends to replicate among applicants the ethnicity of business owners and their initial employees. The second section of chapter 3 presents evidence that entrepreneurship and unemployment are negatively correlated across demographic groups. The ethnic composition of employees tends to reflect that of the owners.

Chapters 4 through 6 turn to antidiscrimination policy. Chapter 4 begins with an overview of employment discrimination law in the United States. My experience as an expert witness in discrimination litigation informs a hands-on discussion of the statistical and economic analysis that is a common component of allegations that minority, female, or older job seekers were systematically excluded from consideration for employment. Class action lawsuits alleging recruitment discrimination often include a determination of "availability"—the representation of blacks, women, and so forth among those qualified for and potentially interested in a firm's jobs. Census data can provide availability benchmarks for minority and female, but not older, job seekers.

When plaintiffs present well-founded statistical and economic arguments, defendant employers must justify their recruitment and hiring patterns on grounds of business necessity. These concepts are well illustrated by a federal case, *Equal Employment Opportunity Commission v. O&G Spring and Wire Forms Specialty Company,* originally heard prior to the Supreme Court's landmark *Wards Cove* decision and reheard thereafter.

The last section of chapter 4 includes a critique of the U.S. Department of Labor's affirmative action availability methodology developed for federal contractors. Not only does the Labor Department require use of an ill-conceived set of "Eight Factors" that is at odds with correct availability determination, but its regulators apply a measure of minority and female "underutilization" that is unrealistically strict and contrary to standard statistical methodology accepted by federal courts and other government agencies.

Policy recommendations vis-à-vis employment discrimination can be based on theoretical or empirical considerations. Chapter 5 addresses the former, first discussing how economists analyze policy options, and then focusing specifically on efficiency and equity implications of employment discrimination policy. On balance, arguments for antidiscrimination intervention are stronger for public than private employers; for large than small establishments; and for groups with high unemployment rates than for those well off. The observation that members of a given minority group will be able to prosper so long as only a small subset of employers does not discriminate against them weakens arguments for universal regulatory coverage. The second section of chapter 5, a discussion of the dominant employment discrimination paradigm in economics, notes that the competition between discriminating and nondiscriminating employers presumed eventually to eradicate discrimination ignores the dynamism of an economy in which two competitors are not likely to be locked in long-term economic combat under static conditions.

Chapter 6 interprets empirical studies of the employment effects of federal antidiscrimination and affirmative action regulations. Title VII of the Civil Rights Act of 1964 apparently significantly affected blacks' employment only in the South in the late 1960s and early 1970s, a result consistent with strong effects of desegregation and weak effects of other federal enforcement. The Department of Labor's affirmative action requirements increased federal contractor employment of blacks over that in comparable noncontractor firms. However, given the lack of contraction in black-white unemployment rate differentials in the 1970s and 1980s, a reasonable reconciliation of the evidence is that large firms and federal contractors employ minorities who, in the absence of regulation, would have been hired elsewhere. Additionally, firms seeking to reduce their exposure to litigation have incentives to avoid hiring minority, female, and older applicants. Furthermore, employers of fifteen or fewer—comprising about 20 percent of the private sector work force—are not covered by the Civil Rights Act, and noncontractors with fewer than one hundred employees—a group including about half that work force—do not regularly submit reports monitored by officials in government agencies with authority to file lawsuits.

Expanding antidiscrimination and affirmative action coverage could backfire. Employers can elude stringent regulation by moving offshore, locating in areas with few minorities, or establishing firms of exempt size. Similarly, eliminating antidiscrimination laws might not be terribly detrimental to minority job seekers because employers would no longer have incentives to evade regulation. Moreover, private resources devoted to antidiscrimination and affirmative action compliance could be reallocated to expanding production and jobs, and public program funds to efforts seeking directly to improve minorities' labor market status.

At any rate, the discussion suggests that reducing minority unemployment requires policies other than those emphasizing employment discrimination. After reviewing conventional unemployment remedies, chapter 7 focuses on the impact of drugs, crime, job location, and the low rate of minority business formation on inner-city employment. In the hope of encouraging new approaches, the last section of the chapter discusses how linking job seekers and employers needing short-term help could improve minorities' long-term employment prospects.

In anticipation of a diverse audience including students, human resources professionals, and attorneys, I have defined economic and statistical terms, explained calculations, and, in general, provided more discussion than would be necessary if readers were limited to social scientists. At the same time, the book proposes several hypotheses, statistical examination of which can determine whether and to what extent they predict the behavior of employers, employees, and job seekers.

CHAPTER TWO

Recruitment Practices

Twenty-five hundred years ago, the Colonos, an area within Athens' Agora, was reserved for men seeking work.[1] Today, contractors still dispatch agents to designated street corners and rural crossroads throughout the world to collect dayworkers. Yet modern employers have available an array of recruitment practices by which to generate job applicants. Understanding these is crucial to appreciating chapter 3's discussion of intentional and unintentional recruitment discrimination.

Recruitment is costly. Employers pay to place their prepared advertisements of job vacancies with newspapers and employment agencies, and allocate time to screening and evaluating applicants by interviewing and testing them, checking references, and reviewing written material. Ad preparation is a strategic function that can be likened to marketing, while identification and qualification of potential applicants is similar to the initial stages of sales.

Similarly, job seekers allocate time to reading and responding to help-wanted ads, visiting work sites and employment agencies, and discussing job opportunities. That these activities are more practicable for unemployed persons than for those at work is a keystone of the original search theory literature's implications for trade-offs between unemployment and inflation.[2] Analogously to employers, job seekers engage in the marketing process of preparing one or more information packages including résumés, transcripts, writing samples, and lists of references; as well as the sales activity of circulating these data to potential employers.

By considering as serious applicants only those who submit specific application forms and perhaps other required material such as writing samples or

1. Tomás Martinez, *The Human Marketplace: An Examination of Private Employment Agencies* (New Brunswick, N.J.: Transaction Books, 1976), p. 7.
2. See Edmund S. Phelps, ed., *Microfoundations of Employment and Inflation Theory* (New York: Norton, 1970).

transcripts, employers can differentiate bona fide applicants from the larger set of individuals who express interest in their jobs. Employers can choose not to accept applications unless they have current job vacancies, or to retain applications for a time in anticipation of future job openings. *Serious* applicants, who submit proper materials, may or may not be *qualified* applicants, those able to perform the employers' jobs.

In an environment where employment decisions are regulated and litigated, distinguishing serious job applicants from others is not merely an academic exercise. Applicant recordkeeping requirements—such as those in force in the United States—will clearly be a less onerous burden on employers the more narrowly applicants are defined. And as noted in subsection 4.2.1, employment discrimination allegations can be supported or refuted with the same employer during the same time period depending on the definition of "applicant."

Employers may not accept applications from blacks, women, or others, or, similarly to differential enforcement of voter literacy requirements, may demand from them especially detailed applications or tighter time limits within which to submit materials. These and related practices are illegal under anti-discrimination law in the United States (see chapter 4).

The policy of requiring applicants to submit salary histories allows employers to screen job seekers whose expectations of salary appear to be higher than that which the employer wants to offer or so low as to suggest insufficient applicant qualifications.[3] Theoretically, salary histories obviate wage surveys or other studies to determine appropriate pay scales.[4]

Employers have many available methods to recruit hires, and job seekers many ways to look for work. Word-of-mouth recruitment, drawing applicants from the personal contacts of business owners and their employees, is the

---

3. This policy is the reverse of an employer's advertisement of a wage rate to attract only applicants who believe their productivity to be congruent with that wage. Such an advertising policy reflects the sorting function of "efficiency wages," pay set above market-clearing levels to attract superior workers, increase productivity, reduce turnover, and, in less developed countries, provide earnings sufficient to maintain workers' nutrition and health. See Andrew Weiss, *Efficiency Wages: Models of Unemployment, Layoffs, and Wage Dispersion* (Princeton, N.J.: Princeton University Press, 1990), esp. chap. 1.

4. In fact, a blind ad (not revealing the employer's identity) asking for salary histories may appear to be a clever way not only to avoid a potentially costly wage survey but also to determine a pay level to be advertised in a future ad in which the employer's identity is revealed. However, it is most unlikely that employers ever use this ruse. First, an ad sufficiently detailed to attract responses from the type of applicants in whom an employer would be interested would probably be so similar to the future, more explicit ad that some job applicants would notice the similarity and react adversely to the employer's secretive strategy. Furthermore, ads themselves are costly, in terms of both explicit monetary costs of placing the ad in a publication and, usually more important, employee time involved in designing the ad and analyzing the responses to it. Finally, unless they are moving into a new area with jobs not similar to those already there, employers usually have a good idea of prevailing pay rates for their jobs.

subject of section 2.1. Employees so recruited will tend to realize above-average productivity, pay, and job stability. Other in-house recruitment methods on which firms can rely—placing classified ads, accepting direct applications from walk-ins, enlisting employment agencies, and utilizing targeted recruitment policies (by which members of some ethnic groups are more likely than others to learn of job vacancies)—are discussed in the second section of this chapter. Not addressed are recruitment activities, such as participation in school career days, that publicize an employer, but are not directed at filling specific vacancies.

Alternatives to in-house recruitment include the retention of temporary help agencies and business services. As discussed in this chapter's third section, these specialized institutions can provide significant cost savings for employers.

Section 2.4 is a discussion of *initial* applicant evaluation, emphasizing employers' summary rejection of those whose application forms indicate spotty work histories, residences far from the work site, criminal convictions, or any other characteristics employers associate with a low likelihood of productive, stable employment. Finally, this chapter's last section is a summary of empirical studies of the use and efficacy of job seekers' search methods.

An alternative to recruiting new hires is overtime work for current employees. In the United States, overtime hours are paid at higher than standard hourly rates—usually at one and one-half times standard pay ("time and a half")—when workers are "nonexempt," i.e., covered by the Fair Labor Standards Act (FLSA). For salaried, usually higher-paid, employees exempt from FLSA coverage, a certain amount of work beyond the standard forty-hour week is often expected, with salary for similar jobs across employers presumably correlated with usual weekly hours of work. Sometimes a great deal of overtime is rewarded with "comp time," allowing employees to take time off later with no loss in pay.

At some point, hiring an additional employee will be less costly than assigning overtime work for current employees—even including the attendant recruitment, hiring, and employment costs such as placing help-wanted ads, evaluating applicants, and providing fringe benefits for those hired. The greater the overtime premium, the greater employers' incentives to hire new employees rather than to incur overtime hours for those already employed. Nonetheless, economists generally do not advocate increasing the overtime premium to encourage new hires (or the similar policy of restricting weekly hours to spread the available work among more employees).[5]

5. See Fred Best, *Work Sharing: Issues, Policy Options, and Prospects* (Kalamazoo, Mich.: W. E. Upjohn Institute for Employment Research, 1981), and Ronald G. Ehrenberg and Paul L. Schumann, *Longer Hours or More Jobs? An Investigation of Amending Hours Legislation to Create Employment* (Ithaca, N.Y.: New York State School of Industrial and Labor Relations, 1982). The employment effect of increased overtime premiums or shorter work weeks is muted because, in response to increased hourly labor costs (either higher overtime premiums or fixed employee

2.1 Word-of-Mouth Recruitment

Word-of-mouth recruitment involves personal referrals of job seekers to employers by employees, business associates, and others acquainted with both. Knowledge of job opportunities need not be widely disseminated; vacancies often are publicized in writing only on company bulletin boards, or merely discussed within the firm. Alternative methods of announcing job openings, such as newspaper ads or posted help-wanted signs, also will attract many applicants previously unknown to a company's employees and business associates.

Employers often have sufficient information about friends, relatives, and others they know to decide whether these individuals would be suitable employees. If so, employers can offer them jobs with minimal recruitment and evaluation costs. It is in general difficult to determine when employers are extending job offers out of nepotism, to reward friends, or to keep peace in their families, rather than to minimize recruitment and hiring costs.

Job seekers have corresponding interests in obtaining maximum information about prospective employers with minimum investments of their own time. Even when job duties, like those of checkers in supermarkets, are familiar to most prospective applicants, and employment terms and conditions, like hours of work and starting pay, are easy to understand, uncertainty remains about such factors as the personalities of managers and coworkers. This uncertainty is minimized when applicants know current employees (including managers), and can be relatively low when applicants have contacts who know them. Thus, personal referrals require relatively little information acquisition by both employers and job seekers.

Those hired via word-of-mouth recruitment may be especially productive workers. To take an extreme example, in a multilingual society, word-of-mouth recruitment may attract only applicants and new hires who speak the same language as the employer and the firm's current employees, and communication on the job may be much easier than it would be if the new hire spoke another language. Indeed, differences in language and culture may render even employee evaluation so difficult that only applicants in the same subculture as that of the employer can be properly assessed. Less drastically, cultural commonalities other than language may have similar productivity-augmenting effects by increasing the comfort of those working together.

The situation in which employers already know job applicants may be closely approximated when applicants are referred by employers' friends,

---

costs such as fringe benefits spread over fewer hours per week), firms would cut back on production and substitute capital for labor, while some employees formerly working overtime or longer work weeks would seek moonlighting jobs that others would have held had the work week not been reduced. Furthermore, the unemployed do not always have the same skills as those originally working overtime or longer work weeks.

business associates, or current employees. Mindful that an employer's unfortunate experience with a new hire could adversely affect the relationship between the employer and the individual referring that hire, sources will tend not to propose poorly qualified candidates. Recommendations will be more useful, the easier it is to judge job seekers' qualifications. Thus, an employer's friends may be able to recommend applicants for laborer jobs if they can vouch for their responsibility and physical fitness, but not for positions as computer programmers if determining programming competence is beyond their ken.

Employers may solidify relationships with business associates by hiring their referrals. The productivity of employees so referred is not limited to their direct contribution to company output, but also reflects their role in increasing the probability of acquiring or maintaining the account of the customer who referred them. Similarly, current employees may provide their newly hired friends with informal on-the-job training beyond that which would ordinarily be given, or may work more efficiently with their friends than with others, thereby increasing the productivity of these new hires over that of those otherwise recruited. Moreover, employees personally referred to an employer have additional incentives to work hard so as not to embarrass those who referred them. Finally, hiring neighbors may reduce new hires' explicit commuting costs (if they car pool), increase their enjoyment (or reduce the discomfort) of commuting, and increase their ability to discuss work after hours. Bonuses paid to employees who refer new hires reflect both the employer's avoidance of recruitment costs necessary initially to attract new hires and expected above-average productivity of those so recruited. A policy of paying bonuses only if the new hire is employed for a stated length of time particularly encourages referrals of job seekers who will perform competently and not soon seek other employment.

Word-of-mouth networks are limited by the contacts of employers, their employees, and business associates. As firms grow, so does the number of employees who can refer new applicants. However, because neither the extent of business contacts nor the number of managers and on-site owners—whose interest in recruiting is generally stronger than that of other employees—tends to expand as fast as firm size, large firms will be more likely than small ones to exhaust their word-of-mouth networks. Consequently, with similar turnover rates (annual job separations divided by the number of incumbent employees), small firms may be able to fill their limited vacancies through word-of-mouth referrals, while larger firms may have to avail themselves of other recruitment methods. As a result, the proportion of employees recruited via word of mouth is likely to be greater, the smaller a firm's number of hires—or, assuming similar turnover rates across large and small firms, employees. This proposition is supported in a study of newly hired professionals, managers, and technicians.[6]

In large organizations, those with hiring authority rarely work closely with most employees or business associates recommending job candidates. Thus, these job seekers' rejecting or not receiving employment offers less likely will cause friction between employers and references than in small establishments and firms where hiring authority is vested in employees who interact frequently with those referring potential hires. It follows that word-of-mouth recruits are more apt to be hired in small than in large firms to enhance good working and customer relations. In addition, new hires in large firms have slight prospects of working directly with the employees who referred them. Consequently, small rather than large firms will tend to benefit from the higher productivity of word-of-mouth recruits who apply themselves especially diligently so as not to embarrass those who referred them and who work directly—and relatively productively—with friends. These considerations reinforce the propensity of small firms to recruit via word of mouth.

The above discussion suggests at least five hypotheses that can be examined statistically:

1. The more complex the job (complexity may be proxied by the rate of pay, or the required education or experience), the lower will be the proportion of employees recruited through personal referrals. The duties of complex jobs and the ability of job seekers to perform them are relatively difficult for many references to assess.
2. For several reasons, the productivity level and productivity increases of new hires (which may be measured directly or proxied by increases in pay during the first year of employment) will be greater for those referred via word of mouth than for those otherwise recruited.
3. In particular, the productivity increase of a new hire will be greater, the greater the representation of friends among immediate coworkers (or the greater the representation of members of the same ethnic, language, or racial group among immediate coworkers).
4. The rate of pay will be lower for employees who work with or near neighbors with whom they can commute (including neighbors employed in nearby firms and in firms that are not close but on the same commuting path), independently of whether these neighbors have referred the employees or even work in the same establishment. This proposition follows from employees' being willing to take lower pay in jobs for which their pecuniary commuting costs are lower or nonpecuniary commuting benefits (e.g., being able to converse with a friend en route between home and work) are higher.

6. Mark S. Granovetter, *Getting a Job: A Study of Contacts and Careers* (Cambridge, Mass.: Harvard University Press, 1974), p. 128. Large firms were defined in this study as those with one hundred or more employees.

5. Employee turnover rates will be relatively low for those who work with or near neighbors (used inclusively as in 4), or who were recruited through personal referrals, or who have friends (or members of the same ethnic group) among their coworkers. Those who work with or near neighbors will tend to have lower commuting costs (including lower net costs after accounting for higher nonpecuniary commuting benefits), and therefore the equivalent of higher pay than their direct compensation suggests; the equivalent of higher pay will discourage quits. The relatively higher productivity of those recruited through personal referrals or working with friends (see 2 and 3 above) will discourage both layoffs and, because productivity increases pay, quits.

Each of these hypotheses presumes that other relevant factors are held constant. For example, hypothesis 1 states that the proportion of hires recruited through personal referrals will vary inversely with job complexity. Proposed earlier was the negative correlation between the proportion of hires recruited by personal referrals and firm size. Thus, a researcher would examine the percentage of hires recruited via word of mouth across a set of firms as a function of both job complexity and firm size (as well as other factors representing the heterogeneity of employers in the study). If the proportion of hires recruited by word of mouth was negatively associated with job complexity, holding constant firm size and the other factors, hypothesis 1 above would be supported.

Furthermore, some of the variables in these hypotheses may be simultaneously determined. Hypothesis 5 posits a negative relationship between utilization of word-of-mouth recruitment and employee turnover. At the same time, firms with little turnover may be able to fill all their vacancies via word of mouth. A negative correlation between the incidence of word-of-mouth recruitment and employee turnover across firms reflects both of these effects. Research testing hypothesis 5 should focus instead on turnover rates of employees alternatively recruited within the same establishment.

I do not believe that the five hypotheses listed above have been previously proposed, let alone investigated. Nonetheless, some support for hypotheses 1, 4, and 5 can be found in the economics literature. In one survey, employers were more likely to recruit specifically for jobs that were white collar or required a great deal of education or on-the-job training. Although the definition of "recruiting" was not clear, to the extent "not recruiting" meant accepting word-of-mouth referrals, in contrast to more formally announcing job vacancies, the pattern would be consistent with hypothesis 1's negative association between job complexity and the incidence of word-of-mouth recruitment.[7]

---

7. See p. 50 in John M. Barron, John Bishop, and William C. Dunkelberg, "Employer Search: The Interviewing and Hiring of New Employees," *Review of Economics and Statistics* 67: 1 (February 1985): 43–52.

A positive association between hourly earnings and the distance employees travel to work has been established in several studies.[8] Rather than measuring the ease of commutes only by distance from work or commuting time, the formulation presented in hypothesis 4 includes as a dimension of commuting cost the company of neighbors. The generalization of commuting cost beyond price and time to the convenience of traveling with neighbors is akin to the generalization of the cost of consumer goods beyond price to such factors as the time required to shop.

Finally, hypothesis 5 is supported by a study concluding that employees with prehire contacts at their workplace had significantly lower quit rates than others.[9] Interestingly, knowing "someone with say" at the firm did not significantly affect quits, thus suggesting that the benefits of working with compatible colleagues rather than knowing someone with clout lowered employees' propensity to quit. Informal contacts especially lowered the quit rate for college graduates and blacks. Relative to high school graduates and whites, these groups would be expected to have, respectively, relatively complex jobs and great uncertainty about the level of comfort with presumably mostly nonblack coworkers. For each group, then, the ability to learn details about a new job before accepting an employment offer was particularly useful in determining the probability of a good job match.

In sum, word-of-mouth recruitment is a method of attracting few applicants with relatively rich prehire information and, if employed, above-average productivity, especially in smaller firms. Although employees so referred will be able to fill most or all vacancies in establishments with few employees and/or low turnover, their high productivity and low evaluation costs suggest that they will be most welcome job candidates even when employers enlist other recruitment practices to generate the bulk of their applicants.

2.2 Other Recruitment Practices

When personal referrals cannot provide a sufficient number of applicants, employers and prospective employees must find each other via alternative methods. Applicants—and, to a lesser and varying extent, employers—initially need to convey more information than is generally the case with personal referrals. Furthermore, the very existence of job vacancies must be publicized beyond an employer's current work force and business associates.

8. See, for example, pp. 169–75 in Albert Rees and George P. Shultz, *Workers and Wages in an Urban Labor Market* (Chicago: University of Chicago Press, 1970), a detailed study of the Chicago-area labor market.

9. Linda Datcher, "The Impact of Informal Networks on Quit Behavior," *Review of Economics and Statistics* 65: 3 (August 1983): 491–95.

2.2.1 Classified Advertisements

Perhaps the most common method of formally announcing job vacancies is placement of classified help-wanted advertisements in local major daily newspapers. These newspapers are more widely circulated than those whose readership is limited to residents of city neighborhoods or suburbs, or targeted at ethnic communities; and ads therein potentially can reach all job seekers who can read or find someone to read to them.

Employers whose job offers to those in high-prestige, high-paying occupations can induce long-distance moves will have limited success with local newspaper ads that reach only those residing in that paper's circulation zone. Superior alternatives include newspapers with national circulation and professional journals whose readership includes a substantial number of those capable of performing the given jobs.

Just as all but the highest-paying jobs are generally not attractive enough to encourage moves from one metropolitan area to another, so part-time and other occasional jobs as well as low-wage full-time employment may not draw commuters from outside a neighborhood or small town. For these jobs, an alternative to placing advertisements in an area's major daily newspapers is placing similar advertisements in city neighborhood or suburban papers. Because of the limited circulation of smaller papers, their ads are generally less expensive. Their small readership, their primary disadvantage, may present no problem if ads generate a sufficient number of qualified applicants. Also, a common presumption is that, compared with those with longer commutes, workers living nearby are not as likely to be absent or tardy, or to quit because another job's location is more convenient. And employers may be able to avoid paying the higher wages putatively associated with longer commutes (see section 2.1) if they hire locally.

2.2.2 Walk-Ins

Help-wanted signs in store windows have much in common with neighborhood newspaper ads. Both will be seen almost exclusively by those who live or work in the area. Even with no help-wanted signs or other job advertisement, large well-known employers may receive inquiries from job seekers who walk in hoping to find vacancies. Employers can choose to accept or to reject applications if they have no current vacancies, and to give walk-ins varying amounts of information about expected future vacancies and job qualifications.

It is clearly reasonable for job seekers to investigate the potentially greater number of employment possibilities at large rather than small firms, just as apartment hunters are well advised (ignoring residential preferences) to search large complexes rather than buildings with only a few units. Indeed, it may be largely futile to seek jobs at small firms not advertising vacancies, just as it would not be efficient to canvass apartments in small buildings or rooms in houses, most of which, in the absence of ads seeking tenants, will not have units available for rent. These considerations suggest the testable hypothesis that the proportion of applicants who apply directly as walk-ins will be greater, the larger the employer, a pattern observed in one study of professionals, managers, and technicians.[10]

Although walk-ins are predominantly those visiting work sites, job seekers may also encounter prospective employers elsewhere—on the street, at social events, or after religious services. New jobs can also be discovered while working, although business accounts may be jeopardized if hiring someone else's employee is interpreted as "raiding." In particular, part-time or seasonal workers may be seeking complementary jobs. For example: "One small firm hired its accountants through the public accounting firm that audited its books. A distributor of furniture and home appliances hired warehousemen through moving and storage companies, whose slack season coincided with his busy season."[11]

2.2.3 Employment Agencies

Some employers forward notices of their job vacancies to organizations whose purposes include publicizing employment opportunities to job seekers. Perhaps the most efficient of these organizations are trade union hiring halls, which refer their members to employers requiring specific skills, most notably in the construction trades. Like crews assembled by labor contractors, workers recruited through hiring halls are normally working at temporary assignments.

Other employers enlist private or public employment agencies, institutions with a venerable history:

> One of the earliest examples of job middlemen occurs in Ancient Sumer. The job middlemen were actually temple priests who would enroll and dispatch laborers and servants for temporary employment in neighboring areas. During this period Sumerian priests comprised the ruling elite. A primary concern of the governing body was building "public projects." The need for a steady supply of workers coincided with the development of a more efficient means of processing laborers. By converting their temples into employment agencies and the priests into employment agents, the ruling elite in ancient Sumer enacted an administrative solution to the recruitment problem.[12]

10. Granovetter, *Getting a Job*, p. 128.
11. Rees and Shultz, *Workers and Wages in an Urban Labor Market*, p. 203.
12. Martinez, *The Human Marketplace*, p. 9.

Today, private employment agencies are often specialized by occupation. Their detailed knowledge of specific labor markets allows them to assess in some detail the capabilities of individual job seekers and their suitability for clients' job vacancies.

Agencies specializing in professional and managerial employees are known as search firms, executive recruiters, and, less flatteringly, "headhunters." These firms customarily receive compensation from employers only if they produce someone who is ultimately hired, although some bill as well or instead for hours they work on behalf of an employer client. Some are remunerated by job seekers.

In contrast, public or community agencies are usually not-for-profit organizations funded publicly and privately through grants and contributions. Unlike most private employment agencies, they commonly provide counseling for job seekers to enhance their "employability."[13] The U.S. Department of Labor's Employment and Training Administration allocates funds from employers' unemployment insurance payments to state employment security agencies to operate almost two thousand Employment Service offices that assist job seekers and employers in filling permanent vacancies.[14] Community employment agencies are apt to specialize by race, ethnicity, sex, or age; employers wishing to recruit members of specific racial or ethnic groups can target their recruitment efforts at the appropriate community organizations.

Many other organizations can refer job seekers to employers. Job announcements can be posted at military bases for armed forces personnel when they leave the service, and members of their families before that. Public and private schools and training programs can place their students in part-time employment while enrolled and full-time employment after graduation. And some employers provide outplacement assistance for their newly terminated employees.

2.2.4 Targeted Recruitment

Employers have considerable ability to target their recruitment efforts at subsets of those who would be interested in their jobs. Placing ads in ethnic newspapers, informing community leaders of job openings, and posting notices at religious or fraternal organizations can generate large numbers of applicants from a specific ethnic group, especially if that group's members live near the employer, have relatively high unemployment rates, and command skills corresponding to those required by the jobs.

Help-wanted signs will be seen disproportionately by those living or working in the employer's immediate area, and therefore can serve as an intentional

---

13. Ibid., chap. 2.

14. U.S. Department of Labor Program Highlights, Fact Sheet No. ETA 90-1, "Employment Service" (Washington: U.S. Department of Labor, 1990).

or unintentional demographic targeting device. Searching for workers with particular skills also may involve unintentional ethnic targeting: An employer seeking college students can place ads in college publications or post signs on campus bulletin boards. If the ethnicity of the student body is not similar to that of the wider labor market from which employees could be drawn, ethnic groups well represented at the college will be disproportionately found among applicants. Similarly, workers laid off by one member of a contractor association would often be excellent candidates for jobs with another contractor in the same association. If historically these contractors have sought workers from particular ethnic groups, then recruiting from this pool of workers will involve targeted ethnic recruitment.

Although societies are typically much more segregated by race, ethnicity, and national origin than by age or sex, opportunities remain to target only males or females, or those in specific age ranges. Employers can target younger workers by directing advertising to trade schools, adult education centers, and the like, because even classes for those who have finished their formal education are attended predominantly by younger students. Employers can also target youths with ads on radio stations or bulletin boards in establishments patronized by youngsters. And targeting certain immigrant groups sometimes concomitantly involves targeting young men or young women. The ability to target one sex rather than the other through ads is perhaps even more limited than the ability to do so by age. However, publications directed at men or women, and single-sex clubs and associations, permit targeting to men rather than women, or vice versa.

Targeted recruitment can also be defined as filling specific job vacancies with members of different groups—for example, having separate sales teams of Anglo whites, blacks, and Hispanics. This blatant ethnic hiring is illegal under the employment discrimination laws reviewed in section 4.1. Nonetheless, in addition to the benefits of homogeneous teams emphasized in the above discussion of word-of-mouth recruitment, the esprit de corps of competing teams conceivably could sublimate ethnic rivalry into high-level production.

2.3 Alternatives to In-House Recruitment

Instead of recruiting and hiring permanent employees, employers can rely on temporary help agencies and firms providing business services. Like private employment agencies that perform screening functions, these organizations save employers recruitment and evaluation costs,[15] and reduce pay and fringe benefit expenses.

15. Recruitment and evaluation services are but two of many functions that can be performed internally or externally. The original paper on the decision of whether to produce goods and services within or without a firm is R. H. Coase, "The Nature of the Firm," *Economica* vol. 4 (n.s.), no. 16 (November 1937): 386–405.

Temporary workers and employees of business services, along with part-time and self-employed workers, constitute a rapidly growing segment of the American labor force: Between 1980 and 1988, the number of temporary workers increased from 400,000 to 1.1 million; employees of business services firms increased from 3.3 million to 5.6 million.[16]

2.3.1 Temporary Help Agencies

Temporary help agencies have a crew of workers and a clientele of employers who may need these workers at short notice or for a limited term of employment. Because agencies normally will have a longer relationship with their temporary employees than will any employer client,[17] agencies will find it less costly than employers to invest in recruitment and evaluation functions. Agencies also save employer clients costs of "hoarding" labor, that is, keeping unneeded workers on payrolls so they will be available later: If an employer is not certain during which weeks in the next three months it will need a worker, paying that worker for the entire three-month period will be very costly. Additionally, agencies save employers recordkeeping and payroll expenses: Employers pay agencies a lump sum, and agencies issue separate checks to temporaries, deduct income taxes, contribute to Social Security, and disburse other funds.[18]

In the last decade, the temporary help industry has begun to train its workers, especially in the use of modern office equipment. Some agencies also provide health insurance and other benefits for their temporaries, who rarely receive such coverage from the agencies' employer clients.[19]

Because temporary help agencies solve the problem of employers' imperfect forecasting of their demand for labor, save them costs of hoarding labor, and assume the recruitment and applicant evaluation functions, some premium charged by temporary help agencies over and above the market wage for the same employees working permanently is well deserved. Correspondingly, temporary help agencies must charge premium pay for the employees they

16. Richard S. Belous, *The Contingent Economy: The Growth of the Temporary, Part-Time, and Subcontracted Workforce* (Washington: National Planning Association, 1989), table 2.1, p. 16. With the 19.8 million part-time and 10.1 million self-employed workers in 1988 (each of which had increased about 20 percent since 1980), contingent workers constituted between 29.9 percent and 36.6 percent of the entire work force in 1988, with the imprecision resulting from an unknown amount of double-counting, e.g., counting twice a temporary worker employed in a business services firm.

17. The exception obtains when employers permanently hire those originally working as temporaries.

18. Likewise, the Sumerian priest–employment agents (see subsection 2.2.3) distributed payments to workers with fees already deducted. See Martinez, *The Human Marketplace,* p. 9.

19. Belous, *The Contingent Economy,* p. 31.

supply to cover agency recruitment, evaluation, and scheduling costs. Thus, supply as well as demand considerations support temporary workers' relatively high pay, which is divided between agencies and temporary workers.

Temporary help services require either a few firms who retain them frequently or many firms who retain them occasionally. They are thus likely to be found in central business districts of cities rather than in less populated suburbs, small towns, or rural areas. Furthermore, they are likely to have employees available for work during the time their clients are generally open for business, namely, standard "nine to five," Monday through Friday hours.

2.3.2 Business Services

An alternative to temporary help agency referrals or permanent employees are firms that provide such business services as computer and data processing, credit reporting and collection, and clerical support. Employers who need these services may find it more profitable to use existing firms than to hire employees as messengers, clerks, et cetera, just as other employers find it preferable to use temporary agencies and search firms than to recruit using their own personnel. Some employers patronize business service firms to avoid purchasing equipment such as copying machines. Similarly to temporary help agencies, service firms save employers recruitment, interviewing, and labor hoarding costs, and are more likely to be found in densely populated business areas, to be open during "normal" business hours, and to charge more than a full-time employer would have to pay for the same service: For example, the equivalent hourly pay for a service firm's messenger will exceed that for a comparable messenger employed full-time by an employer not in the courier industry.

Business service firms provide promotional opportunities beyond those available to the same employees working for employers in other industries. A messenger working in a firm specializing in deliveries can advance by supervising messengers, marketing delivery services, and even organizing new establishments.[20] The same messenger hired by a firm in another industry will probably be in a dead-end job. Thus, both the providers and the users of these services have incentives to substitute business for employer-employee relationships.

A hybrid between service firms and temporary help agencies is the provision by temporary help firms of teams to provide services like mailrooms, copy centers, and telephone marketing operations. Contracting services account for an increasing share of temporary help firms' business.[21]

20. See Peter Drucker, "Sell the Mailroom," *Wall Street Journal,* July 25, 1989, p. A18.
21. Steve Lohr, "More Workers in the U.S. Are Becoming Hired Guns," *New York Times,* August 14, 1992, p. A1.

Small and medium-sized firms will tend to be primary clients of service firms because the level of business in large firms may be sufficient to afford hiring, say, a full-time messenger in-house. Large firms have many opportunities to hire temporary workers, but less need to hire temporaries to avoid labor hoarding: A firm with work for 100 secretaries full-time will employ 101 or more secretaries, in view of the likelihood that one or more secretaries will be absent on any given day. In a small firm with enough work for only one secretary, it would be wasteful to have a second secretary on board—double the labor—to cover when the primary secretary is absent. Instead, it is worth using a temporary help agency for perhaps several days per year to cover the primary secretary's vacations, occasional absences, and higher than normal workloads. Consequently, an increasing number of small firms and fewer mergers and acquisitions of them are positive developments for business service firms and perhaps for temporary help agencies.

2.4 Initial Applicant Evaluation

Employers learn about applicants during initial discussions on the phone and in person, or from quick scans of submitted application forms and résumés. Because it is time-consuming to evaluate all possible job candidates, employers adopt the practice of summarily rejecting certain applicants.

An application form usually includes space for an applicant's name, address, educational background, work history, conviction record, foreign language competence, hobbies, and references. Consistent with the antidiscrimination laws to be discussed in chapter 4, race, sex, age, and marital status are not explicitly included on these forms, except perhaps on tear sheets that allow employers to record and to tabulate the race and sex of their applicants, and which are removed before being seen by company officials responsible for hiring decisions. Data on application forms or résumés—especially names, addresses, dates, and schools attended—may of course strongly suggest race, ethnicity, sex, or age as well as marital status, an area that employers are advised not to probe lest they illegally invoke stereotypes about married women's commitment to the labor force. Applicant information allows employers to cull only members of certain demographic groups in an attempt either to maintain homogeneous work forces for the reasons noted in section 2.1 or to discriminate for any of the reasons to be discussed in chapter 3.

The appearance of application forms may influence some employers, particularly in clerical or other jobs where neatness is valued. Inapt entries and misspellings signal language difficulties that can impede performance of all but extreme rote tasks. Incomplete applications suggest an inability to follow directions, or a lack of experience or qualifications to present.

Applications submitted later than most may be interpreted as weak interest in the job opportunity, or lack of initiative that will generalize to on-the-job performance. In any case, employers may tend to make disproportionately many offers to those who apply early because of uncertainty about the qualifications of future applicants and a desire to limit the amount of time spent interviewing and otherwise evaluating candidates.[22]

With respect to the actual content of application forms or résumés, employers may reject candidates because their educational background is insufficient, or so far above requirements as to suggest that they would be accepting jobs solely to provide income while they continue searching for better opportunities. These applicants, expected to be only short-term employees, are classified as "overqualified." A common job requirement is a high school diploma, with a four-year college degree regarded as evidence of overqualification, but some college acceptable, perhaps even desirable.

Work histories are evaluated in many dimensions. Are prior jobs similar to that in which applicants are now interested? Did they require the same skills? For other than entry-level jobs, do applicants present evidence of increasing responsibility over time? Or rather patterns of short job tenure, frequent terminations, and repeated periods of unemployment?[23]

Hobbies may indicate skills similar to those required by some jobs. Thus, applicants who enjoy do-it-yourself projects may have an advantage in competing for jobs requiring mechanical ability. Applicants who can participate on company athletic teams or in other activities may be more appealing to some employers than otherwise similar job candidates.

Many employers will immediately reject applicants with criminal convictions. It will generally be inefficient to investigate these convictions, given the alternative of many applicants without criminal records, and the time-consuming nature and difficulty of examining the crime(s) committed, the extent of rehabilitation, and the likelihood of a relationship of these crimes to job performance.

References may be especially helpful if they are present or former employees, business associates, or others known to the employer. Such references would be expected to furnish candid evaluations, and applicants with positive

22. A result from auctions may have implications for hiring. That higher prices are paid for homogeneous goods, the earlier in the auction the goods are offered for sale, has been observed for wine and real estate. See Orley Ashenfelter and David Genesove, "Testing for Price Anomalies in Real-Estate Auctions," *American Economic Review* 82: 2 (May 1992): 501–5. The direct labor market analogue to this observation is higher pay for earlier than later applicants. When pay is the same for all new hires, this effect shows up in accepting lower qualifications for earlier than later applicants, a special case of which is early applicants being hired when otherwise similar later applicants are not.

23. See John Ballen and Richard B. Freeman, "Transitions between Employment and Non-Employment," pp. 75–112 in Richard B. Freeman and Harry J. Holzer, eds., *The Black Youth Employment Crisis* (Chicago: University of Chicago Press, 1986), esp. table 2.8, p. 94, for summaries of employer interviews indicating negative reactions to applicants' casual work histories, frequent job changes, and many spells of unemployment.

recommendations from trusted sources enjoy significant advantages over other job candidates. At the other extreme, the absence of references may signal a lack of prior employers or others willing to comment favorably on an applicant's ability and skills.

Finally, employers may reject people on the basis of residence, believing that applicants living far away are more likely to be absent and tardy, and more likely to quit upon finding a job nearer their homes.

In tight labor markets, where applicants are few relative to the number of job vacancies, employers may seriously consider applicants whom they would reject in looser labor markets with more unemployed job seekers. In very tight labor markets, job seekers with limited skills may be sought out, and even trained, by employers.

Applicants passing employers' initial screens undergo further evaluation, including interviews; job-related tests; study of the specific tasks for which the employer is hiring; and collection, submission, and review of written material such as references and writing samples. The output of these activities is information about employer and prospective employee ultimately leading to a decision by the employer whether to offer a job, and a decision by the applicant whether and under what terms and conditions to accept a possibly forthcoming job offer. Additional information increases the likelihood of offering a job to a qualified applicant and rejecting an unqualified one. Consequences of hiring unqualified applicants are subpar job performance, termination, and subsequent search for a new employee. Rejecting qualified applicants extends the search period to fill a vacancy, and involves evaluation of more job candidates. Applying the optimality conditions common in economics implies that employers will acquire information about applicants up to the point that the benefit of the additional information in effecting a good job match and avoiding a poor one equals the employer's cost in acquiring that information.

Because it is generally more difficult to effect job matches for complex than for simple jobs, evaluation periods will tend to be longer, the greater the pay and prestige of the position. Thus, hiring an entry-level worker will generally involve a shorter evaluation period than hiring that worker's manager. Indeed, hours spent per applicant recruiting, interviewing, and screening were found to be relatively high for professional and technical jobs, and for jobs requiring a great deal of education or involving substantial on-the-job training.[24] Furthermore, the evaluation period will tend to be longer, the longer the duration of a job. Thus, employers will tend to spend more time interviewing a technician seeking permanent employment than a technician who intends to work only temporarily. Two studies found that employers spent significantly fewer hours

24. Barron, Bishop, and Dunkelberg, "Employer Search," table 2, p. 48. Only the professional/technical indicator and one of the training variables had statistically significant coefficients (i.e., with t-statistics greater than two).

recruiting, interviewing, and evaluating applicants for temporary and seasonal jobs.[25]

Within the category of permanent jobs is an ambiguous relationship between the length of the evaluation period and employee turnover. When turnover—comprising employee-initiated quits and employer-initiated fires—is low, new hires generally remain in their job for a long time and both employers and employees will devote a great deal of attention and effort to forming a relationship they expect to be long-lived. On the other hand, because turnover is costly, it behooves employers to examine applicants especially critically in jobs with a history of high turnover in the hope of effecting a long-term match that will reduce quits and fires. Separations initiated by employers not only may affect the length of the evaluation period but also may be directly inhibited by the costs incurred in replacing discharged employees. Across employers, hours spent recruiting, screening, and interviewing each applicant were not correlated with firm quit rates.[26]

In general, recruitment and hiring costs per new hire will be lower for large than for otherwise similar small firms. One reason is that large firms can exploit economies of scale: The cost of recruiting and hiring two similar employees is less than double and sometimes not much more than the cost of recruiting and hiring one. For example, an advertisement to attract two new hires costs no more than the same ad to attract one. And interviewing two people for the same job may take twice as long as interviewing one, but developing interview questions occurs only once and its cost can be spread over many interviewees.

An applicant will more likely be hired in a large firm with a heterogeneous work force and frequent job vacancies than in an otherwise similar small firm with an occasional vacancy requiring specific skills simply because the probabilities of a match are greater, the greater the number of different jobs and the absolute number of job vacancies. While large firms are evaluating candidates primarily for a specific opening, they may secondarily be considering them for other actual and potential vacancies. Large firms often have specialized personnel departments that reflect a division of labor that many small firms may not be able to support.[27]

25. See pp. 377–78 in John Bishop and John M. Barron, "Extensive Search, Intensive Search, and Hiring Costs: New Evidence on Employer Hiring Activity," *Economic Inquiry* 23: 3 (July 1985): 363–82, and table 1, p. 82, in John M. Barron, Dan A. Black, and Mark A. Loewenstein, "Employer Size: The Implications for Search, Training, Capital Investment, Starting Wages, and Wage Growth," *Journal of Labor Economics* 5: 1 (January 1987): 76–89.

26. Barron, Bishop, and Dunkelberg, "Employer Search," table 2, p. 48.

27. This proposition is analogous to that for product markets, the classic exposition of which is book 3, chapter 3, "That the Division of Labour Is Limited by the Extent of the Market," pp. 17–21 in Adam Smith, *An Inquiry into the Nature and Causes of the Wealth of Nations* (New York: Modern Library, 1937).

These points suggest the prediction that, holding other relevant factors constant, the job offer rate per applicant will be greater in large firms, or, equivalently, that the number of applicants per job offer will be lower in large firms. On the other hand, that small firms rely heavily on word-of-mouth recruitment and large firms receive relatively many applications from walk-ins (see sections 2.1 and 2.2) may counter this effect: Word-of-mouth recruits are more likely than others to be hired, and employers accessible to walk-ins receive many applications, both suitable and not. Large firms' generally more attractive pay, fringe benefits, and job security[28] also would be expected to draw more applicants. Moreover, because large employers tend to purchase expensive machinery requiring skilled labor[29] and seek ways to minimize the high costs of monitoring a large, heterogeneous work force, they may search more extensively for high-ability employees by interviewing a greater number of applicants for each vacancy.[30]

Indeed, one study found that "a doubling in the establishment size increases both the number interviewed per offer and the number of applicants per applicant interviewed [i.e., applicants per interviewees] by approximately five percent; thus the number of applicants per offer increases by approximately ten percent." However, in support of the economies-of-scale point, the authors also note that with doubling in the establishment size, "the number of hours spent per applicant unexpectedly [sic] falls by over two percent," and "[t]his could reflect the gains larger firms experience due to individuals specializing in the hiring activity. Or it could be due to the stockpiling of applicants by larger employers."[31] Similarly, another analysis of the same employer survey found "a 10% increase in employer size [to be] associated with a 1.65% increase in the number of applicants screened per position," but an "unanticipated insignificant effect of employer size on the number of hours spent screening each applicant."[32] And further investigation of these data revealed that holding firm size constant, a 10 percent increase in establishment size was associated with approximately a 1.35 percent increase in the number of applications.[33]

28. See Charles Brown, James Hamilton, and James L. Medoff, *Employers Large and Small* (Cambridge, Mass.: Harvard University Press, 1990), chaps. 4–6.

29. See Daniel S. Hamermesh, "Commentary," pp. 383–88 in John J. Siegfried, ed., *The Economics of Firm Size, Market Structure, and Social Performance* (Washington: Federal Trade Commission, 1980).

30. See Barron, Bishop, and Dunkelberg, "Employer Search," p. 44.

31. Bishop and Barron, "Extensive Search," p. 374.

32. Barron, Black, and Loewenstein, "Employer Size," p. 81.

33. See table 3, p. 757, and table 4, p. 762, in Harry J. Holzer, Lawrence F. Katz, and Alan B. Krueger, "Job Queues and Wages," *Quarterly Journal of Economics* 106: 3 (August 1991): 739–68. The tables report estimates of 1.33 percent and 1.37 percent using slightly different procedures (alternative instruments for two-stage least squares estimation).

2.5 The Use and Efficacy of Job-Seeking Methods

Job seekers' search methods have been studied and tabulated more extensively than employers' recruitment practices. Referrals from friends and relatives, and direct applications submitted by walk-ins, both of which are sometimes categorized as informal job seeking, dominate *successful* job-search behavior. For example, in each of thirty studies undertaken between 1947 and 1970, employees more often found their jobs through these methods than through formal channels such as newspaper ads, private employment agencies, and the public employment service.[34] Early investigators of job-search behavior asked employees how they found their jobs. Later studies examined the extent to which job-search behavior varied with job seekers' occupation, education, race, sex, and age.

Some studies focused solely on the use of various job-search methods without tracking which methods led to job offers and acceptances. Residents of poverty areas (defined as Department of Labor concentrated employment program target areas) in Atlanta and Detroit more frequently used the public employment service and community organizations than did residents of nonpoverty areas, who were more likely to contact employers directly or answer newspaper ads. These patterns held within occupational and racial groups. Living in a poverty area was not correlated with the use of either private employment agencies or referrals from relatives. Within poverty areas in six cities, whites, most of whom were Hispanics, were more likely than blacks to contact employers directly and to check with relatives or friends, while blacks were more likely to make use of the public employment service and community organizations.[35]

Job-search behavior of the unemployed displayed some regularities between 1970 and 1982, the last year the U.S. Department of Labor published tabulations of job-search methods. Contacting employers directly tended to decline with age. The public employment service was used more by men than women and by nonwhites[36] than whites. Women placed or answered ads more than men, and men relied on referrals from friends and relatives more than women. Approximately 70 percent of job seekers contacted employers directly, an unknown percentage of whom were informed of job possibilities

34. These studies are listed in the appendix of David W. Stevens, "A Reexamination of What Is Known about Jobseeking Behavior in the United States," pp. 57–104 in *Labor Market Intermediaries* (Washington: National Commission for Manpower Policy Special Report No. 22, 1978).

35. Harvey J. Hilaski, "How Poverty Area Residents Look for Work," *Monthly Labor Review* 94: 3 (March 1971): 41–46.

36. Before 1973, most Labor Department surveys aggregated nonwhite racial minorities into a "black and other" category. Consequently, many pre-1973 studies are not able to identify specific racial groups other than whites.

through acquaintances. Roughly 25 to 30 percent each used ads or the public employment service. About 15 percent followed referrals of friends and relatives, and 5 to 10 percent signed on with private employment agencies. These percentages sum to 140 to 155 percent because many job seekers used more than one search method.[37] Employed persons looking for work had a distribution of job-search activity similar to that of the unemployed, except for far less use of public employment agencies.[38]

About half of the under age forty-five male household heads, female household heads, and working wives heard about their current job through friends and relatives. Furthermore, before being hired, half knew someone who worked for their current employer. In addition, about 40 percent of the men and one-third of the women indicated that someone helped them get their current job. Women were less likely than men to have found their jobs through personal referrals. Black men were more likely than white men to have learned from a friend about their job, to have known someone who worked there, and to have received some help in getting their job, although less likely than white men to have received direct help.[39]

In most other studies, word-of-mouth networks were much more fruitful for whites than blacks, who tended to rely more on newspaper ads and employment agencies. Using the informal-formal distinction introduced at the beginning of this section, nonwhite Chicago-area material handlers and janitors found jobs through formal sources more than twice as often as did whites.[40] Young black and white men had a similar distribution of job-search methods; informal methods accounted for almost 70 percent of the jobs obtained by whites, and 60 percent of those obtained by blacks. However, whites had significantly higher probabilities of receiving job offers, particularly when submitting direct applications.[41]

Informal methods are relatively more common for lower-paying jobs. When employers were asked to rank ten recruitment methods by their importance as a source for finding employees, contacts through friends and relatives and walk-ins were second and fourth for college graduates, second and third for

37. See Thomas F. Bradshaw, "Jobseeking Methods Used by Unemployed Workers," *Monthly Labor Review* 96: 2 (February 1973): 35–40, and *Handbook of Labor Statistics,* Bureau of Labor Statistics Bulletins 1966, 2000, and 2175 (Washington: Government Printing Office, 1977, 1978, and 1983).

38. Carl Rosenfeld, "The Extent of Job Search by Employed Workers," *Monthly Labor Review* 100: 3 (March 1977): 58–62.

39. Mary Corcoran, Linda Datcher, and Greg J. Duncan, "Most Workers Find Jobs through Word of Mouth," *Monthly Labor Review* 103: 8 (August 1980): 33–35.

40. Rees and Shultz, *Workers and Wages in an Urban Labor Market,* p. 203.

41. Harry J. Holzer, "Informal Job Search and Black Youth Unemployment," *American Economic Review* 77: 3 (June 1987): 446–52.

those with some college, and second and first for high school graduates.[42] Similarly, blue-collar workers find 60 to 90 percent of their jobs through informal methods.[43] And a study of Washington, D.C., area job vacancies not requiring high school diplomas observed that only a third of the vacancies are formally advertised, and most are made known to a limited number of potential applicants.[44]

42. See table A3, p. 36, in Jomills Henry Braddock II and James M. McPartland, "How Minorities Continue to Be Excluded from Equal Employment Opportunities: Research on Labor Market and Institutional Barriers," *Journal of Social Issues* 43: 1 (1987): 5–39.

43. Granovetter, *Getting a Job,* p. 5.

44. Marc Bendick, Jr., and Mary Lou Egan, *Jobs: Employment Opportunities in the Washington Area for Persons with Limited Employment Qualifications* (Washington: Greater Washington Research Center, 1988).

CHAPTER THREE

Recruitment Discrimination

Employment discrimination occurs when employers make decisions based on applicant or employee characteristics that are not job-related. Recruitment discrimination takes place when qualified and potentially interested job seekers are not equally likely to discover employment opportunities because of personal characteristics unrelated to qualifications for and interest in the jobs.

This chapter's sections discuss three categories of recruitment discrimination. The first is a straightforward consequence of hiring practices: Employers who do not want to hire members of an ethnic group can refuse to consider their applications. Some employers may believe that members of certain groups are less productive than others, or that it is more difficult to assess their qualifications.

A second type of recruitment discrimination, often unintentional, follows from use of some of the practices discussed in chapter 2, particularly word-of-mouth recruitment, which, given the ethnic stratification of social networks, tends to replicate among applicants and hires the ethnicity of owners and current employees. The third results when employers apply the criteria discussed in section 2.4 to screen applicants.

What are the benefits of recruitment and hiring discrimination? First, employers may simply prefer hiring members of their own or similar ethnic groups, and be willing to suffer decreased profits to indulge their ethnic prejudice. Alternatively, employers may believe that their employees will be more productive if new hires are of the same ethnic group, a proposition that can be viewed as a simple generalization of the productivity gains based on friends working together (see section 2.1). Finally, even when employers and employees have no desire to discriminate on the basis of ethnicity, they may do so if they believe that employing individuals who are not members of customer-approved ethnic groups would cause some consumers to patronize competitors. These propositions are adaptations of those underlying the basic discrimination paradigm in the economics literature.[1]

This chapter focuses on employer policy with no further consideration of whether employers are discriminating to indulge their own tastes, to placate their employees, or to attempt to satisfy their customers. The emphasis is on discrimination by race and ethnicity, with many of the examples involving blacks and whites. Far more empirical work has focused on blacks than on other minorities. Analysis of male-female labor market differences has emphasized pay differentials and occupational segregation. Little research has focused on other groups whose members may be victims of discrimination.

Indeed, employers, employees, or customers may discriminate on grounds of race, sex, age, religion, political preference, veteran status, marital status, sexual orientation, social history or practices, physical disability or appearance, or any other feature that is not directly work-related.[2] Of course, indulging these tastes may be quite costly if an employer is subject to laws prohibiting discrimination. Similarly, employers may not be allowed to hire certain individuals if laws *require* work-force segregation or other forms of discrimination. Nonetheless, employers may rationally choose to violate laws that prohibit or require discrimination if their expected gain from the violation exceeds the expected penalties. Thus, if the profit gained from hiring a minority worker under a regime requiring segregation is $5,000 per year and three $1,000 fines are expected as a result, the annual expected benefit of violating the law is $2,000 ($5,000 minus three times $1,000).[3]

3.1 Hiring Discrimination

Perhaps the most common paradigm of employment discrimination involves an employer and two equally qualified applicants, say, one black and one

1. See Gary S. Becker, *The Economics of Discrimination,* 2d ed. (Chicago: University of Chicago Press, 1971). One of his models assumes that white employers who discriminate against black workers act as if employing a black involves a psychic cost in addition to the explicit monetary wage paid. Consequences of employer discrimination are reductions in the number of blacks hired, and in the amount they are paid relative to comparable white workers. An alternative model postulates a similar psychic cost incurred by white employees if they have black coworkers, and implies segregated work forces. A consumer discrimination model has white customers discriminating against black sellers and willing to buy from them only at lower prices than they would pay for the same goods or services sold by whites. Consumer discrimination lowers the value of the services provided by black employees, and therefore the amount even a nondiscriminating employer would pay them.

2. In some instances these characteristics are accepted as work-related, and no one charges discrimination. For example, a religious organization may seek to hire only its coreligionists to perform ritualistic functions.

3. See Gary S. Becker, "Crime and Punishment: An Economic Approach," pp. 1–54 in Gary S. Becker and William M. Landes, eds., *Essays in the Economics of Crime and Punishment* (New York: Columbia University Press, 1974).

white. Employers wishing to discriminate against blacks will consistently choose the white candidate. A modification of this paradigm takes into account the low likelihood that two candidates will be exactly *equally* qualified, and describes an employer discriminating against blacks as one consistently favoring whites over blacks from a pool of roughly equally qualified applicants.

More subtly, even with no overt animus toward blacks, employers may disproportionately reject black applicants. Some employers may believe that, on average, blacks are less productive than whites, and thereby choose white applicants over apparently similar blacks. Those who believe that blacks and whites are equally productive on average, but who find it relatively difficult or costly to evaluate blacks' productivity, will still disproportionately reject black applicants, for whom the likelihood of incorrect evaluation is high. These phenomena are modeled mathematically in the literature on statistical discrimination.[4]

Analogously, urban taxicab drivers may refuse to pick up blacks because they believe black passengers are less "productive" in the sense that blacks tend to travel to neighborhoods from which it is unlikely to get a return fare. Furthermore, when it is impractical or illegal to inquire about a prospective passenger's destination, i.e., too costly to evaluate a potential fare's "productivity," taxis may pass up black passengers. Thus, for two reasons, a cab driver may lose a profitable black fare going to a destination where other remunerative fares are abundant, just as an employer may overlook a highly productive black job seeker.

Judging individuals by their group membership may be generally efficient for employers, but sometimes induces poor employer decisions, and systematically engenders fewer job opportunities for highly productive members of groups whose productivity employers underestimate or have difficulty evaluating. This phenomenon explains not only some instances of competent blacks faring poorly in the job market and blacks traveling to "productive" locations being ignored by taxi drivers, but law-abiding blacks, particularly young men, being stopped more than their white counterparts by store security guards and police.

4. Edmund S. Phelps, "The Statistical Theory of Racism and Sexism," *American Economic Review* 62: 4 (September 1972): 659–61; Dennis J. Aigner and Glen G. Cain, "Statistical Theories of Discrimination in Labor Markets," *Industrial and Labor Relations Review* 30: 2 (January 1977): 175–87; George J. Borjas and Matthew S. Goldberg, "Biased Screening and Discrimination in the Labor Market," *American Economic Review* 68: 5 (December 1978): 918–22; Matthew S. Goldberg, "Discrimination, Nepotism, and Long-Run Wage Differentials," *Quarterly Journal of Economics* 97: 2 (May 1982): 307–19; Shelly J. Lundberg and Richard Startz, "Private Discrimination and Social Intervention in Competitive Labor Markets," *American Economic Review* 73: 3 (June 1983): 340–47; and Stewart Schwab, "Is Statistical Discrimination Efficient?" *American Economic Review* 76: 1 (March 1986): 228–34. Although these models focus on wage differences across groups, many of their insights are also applicable to hiring decisions.

Such examples are not limited to race and ethnicity. An employer seeking long-term continuous employees may categorically reject women of child-bearing age on grounds that their having children later will involve at least brief interruptions from work. As a result of this policy, the employer will forgo hiring women who will not have children, others whose maternity leaves of absence will be brief, and still others whose above-average productivity will more than compensate for maternity leaves, whether short or long. Women re-acting to this situation by telling employers they do not intend to have children may initially be hired; however, if some of them have children later, employers will ignore female applicant family planning predictions and return to their original policy of not considering female applicants at all.

Similarly, employers may believe that few women and older workers can perform certain physically demanding jobs; categorically not considering them as applicants is more efficient for the employer than trying to discover the few women and older workers who have the physical capabilities of strong and fit young men. In fact, employers can indirectly discourage women and older workers from applying by offering their employees fringe benefit pack-ages relatively unattractive to women or older workers, e.g., little or no mater-nity leave benefits, and retirement plans with vesting provisions older workers are not likely to fulfill.

It has been argued that the adverse effects of judging individual applicants by their group membership can be mitigated to the extent hiring decisions are made because employers face greater difficulties in evaluating applicants of these groups (as opposed to the effects of employer beliefs that these appli-cants are generally less able).[5] First, firms can self-insure against errors by reassigning employees who do not work out (while they benefit from highly productive employees who would have been passed over had their group membership been emphasized). Second, a market for employee tests that are job-related (the classic example being typing tests for typists) will allow ob-jective assessment of applicants. However, these arguments are particularly weak for small firms hiring low-skilled workers. Such firms will have few places to put people who fail in their initial assignments, and often will not be users of tests.

In addition to holding certain beliefs about ability or difficulties in applicant evaluation, some employers may blatantly choose not to accept applications from individuals with certain characteristics that are not work-related. Help-wanted signs stating "Whites Only," "Christians Only," and "No Irish Need Apply" are classic examples that have all but disappeared in the United States because they are so blatantly illegal. Nonetheless, employers may tell female applicants that jobs are only for men; or may inform blacks they have no job

---

5. Aigner and Cain, "Statistical Theories of Discrimination in Labor Markets," pp. 182–83.

vacancies, while distributing application forms to whites inquiring ten minutes earlier or later.

A 1992 study by the Fair Employment Council of Greater Washington involving "applicant testers" illustrates this policy:

> A woman identifying herself as Juanita Alverez [*sic*] called an optometrist's office in suburban Virginia to apply for a receptionist job advertised in a suburban newspaper. She was put on hold for five minutes, called by the name "Carmen" and told that no more applications were being taken.
>
> Thirteen minutes later, another woman with the same qualifications as Alverez, but identifying herself as Julie Ann Mason, called to apply for the job. She was given an appointment for an interview.[6]

How might we explain the optometrist's different treatment of the inquiries of "Ms. Alverez" and "Ms. Mason"? That the optometrist dislikes and does not want to hire Hispanics and so instructs all assistants taking job inquiries, or that some or all of the employees answering the phone in the optometrist's office discriminate against Hispanics, are only two of several possibilities.

Less obviously, in concert with the discussion at the beginning of this section, assume the optometrist is seeking someone with proficiency in using the English language and believes that on average, Hispanics have less command of the English language than others, or that it will be relatively difficult to evaluate Hispanics' language competence. Given that interviews are time-consuming, the optometrist does not wish to interview applicants belonging to a group (Hispanics) whose members are believed to have a lower likelihood of satisfying the job requirements and/or whose job qualifications (fluency in English) will take extra time to assess. The suggestion of less competence in English is supported by the instructions given to the Hispanic testers to "occasionally roll r's [*sic*], shorten vowel sounds . . . and follow Spanish stress patterns."[7]

If Hispanics, particularly those with accents, tend to have less proficiency in the English language than non-Hispanics, not considering Hispanic applicants at all will generally allow the optometrist to find a suitable receptionist with fewer applicant interviews than would be necessary if Hispanics were also to be considered. This policy will of course exclude extremely well-qualified Hispanics, just as an employer hypothetically searching for a tall employee will find it more efficient to interview only men, even though some women are taller than most men. With no general Hispanic versus non-Hispanic difference in qualifications for the receptionist job, and no difference in evaluation

6. Patrice Gaines-Carter, "Hiring Bias Found by Hispanic Testers," *Washington Post*, April 29, 1992, p. C1.

7. Ibid., p. C2.

effort for the two groups, the optometrist's policy will be inefficient by excluding suitable candidates. Nevertheless, the optometrist's belief, rather than the underlying reality, will determine the office's recruitment and hiring policies.

It is also possible that the optometrist or others in the office believe that potential patients will react adversely to a Hispanic receptionist. Patients may believe that it will be more difficult to make appointments with a member of a group whose English-language skills are on average lower than those of others, or that the optometrist for whom the receptionist is working will be more difficult to converse with or otherwise have below-average competence. Alternatively, perhaps predominantly non-Hispanic patients are more comfortable interacting with a receptionist culturally similar to them, thus ruling out Hispanic job candidates.[8] Here, the optometrist's office staff's belief about patients' beliefs determines hiring policy.

Matched pair studies wherein trained "testers" are sent out to apply for jobs[9] have yielded similar results, although sometimes the minority applicant is treated better, and frequently no difference exists. For example, blacks in Chicago and Washington were less likely to be offered jobs or to advance through the applicant evaluation process than similar whites: In 476 hiring audits involving ten pairs of young men, 15 percent of the time the white but not the black, and 5 percent of the time the black but not the white, was offered the job. In the remaining 80 percent of the cases, neither or both received an offer. Also, measuring advancement through the evaluation process by such

8. Differences in communication modalities across groups are akin to language differences. Male-female communication differences are examined at length by Deborah Tannen, *You Just Don't Understand: Women and Men in Conversation* (New York: Morrow, 1990). Kevin Lang, "A Language Theory of Discrimination," *Quarterly Journal of Economics* 101: 2 (May 1986): 363–82, notes that language differences imply segregation not only across firms but also across units within firms. Similar considerations suggest segregation by customers, an example of which in the text is that of non-Hispanic patients preferring offices with non-Hispanic receptionists. In some cases the contrary may hold: Immigrants may feel more acculturated when interacting with natives, and in some instances prefer them to members of their own ethnic group. In addition, members of ethnic groups enjoying reputations for above-average productivity may attract more customers and coworkers.

9. These matched pair experiments have been more common in housing than in employment research, and are beginning to be used to study possible racial bias in loans. See Paulette Thomas, "U.S., Some Bankers Sharply Boost Use of 'Testers' to Find Racial Bias in Loans," *Wall Street Journal,* May 27, 1992, p. B6. Indeed, lawsuits have been successfully brought against apartment houses whose agents told black testers that only some of the apartments on the market, or none, were available. For a discussion of the new role of testers as plaintiffs in employment discrimination litigation, see Fair Employment Council of Greater Washington, Inc., *Annual Report, 1990– 1992,* pp. 10–13. For a presentation of the methodology, as well as the results, of matched pair studies in various markets, see Michael Fix and Raymond J. Struyk, eds., *Clear and Convincing Evidence: Measurement of Discrimination in America* (Washington: Urban Institute Press, 1992).

indicators as being allowed to submit applications or being scheduled for interviews, 20 percent of the time the white advanced further than the black, 7 percent of the time the black advanced further than the white, and in the remaining 73 percent of the cases, both young men were treated similarly.[10]

A related study of 302 hiring audits with eight pairs of Hispanic and Anglo males in Chicago and San Diego resulted in the Anglo only receiving a job offer 22 percent of the time, and the Hispanic only receiving an offer 8 percent of the time, with neither or both receiving an offer in the other 70 percent of the cases. Anglos and Hispanics were advanced more than their matched partner 31 percent and 11 percent of the time, respectively, with similar treatment in the remaining 58 percent of the cases.[11] It is not clear how much of the Hispanic-Anglo differences reflect employer concerns about compliance with the documentation requirements of the 1986 Immigration Reform and Control Act, which involves penalties for employing certain aliens.

These studies can be criticized on several grounds. First, their results cannot be generalized to the extent the employers are not representative of the entire economy. Second, if the testers are attracted to the program by their political orientation, they can engender outcomes suggesting discrimination: Whites can fill in applications neatly, arrive on time, and appear attentive to interviewers; blacks can do the opposite. Third, blacks, Hispanics, and white Anglos may have been preferred by employers with predominantly black, Hispanic, or Anglo work forces to whom the putative applicants would have been similar (see section 3.1). Fourth, for employers covered by antidiscrimination laws, black and Hispanic hires increase the probability of employee-filed lawsuits, while white Anglo hires do not. And fifth, a more pertinent measure of the impact of employment discrimination is not the job offer rate by a single employer but rather employment rates after a sequence of job searches.[12]

At any rate, two researchers obtaining quite frank admissions from employers provide some explanation for the hiring audit patterns: "Our interviews at Chicago-area businesses show that employers view inner-city workers, especially black men, as unstable, uncooperative, dishonest, and uneducated. Race is an important factor in hiring decisions. But it is not race alone: rather it is race in a complex interaction with employers' perceptions of class and space,

10. Margery Austin Turner, Michael Fix, and Raymond J. Struyk, *Opportunities Denied, Opportunities Diminished: Racial Discrimination in Hiring* (Washington: Urban Institute Press, 1991).

11. Harry Cross with Genevieve Kenney, Jane Mell, and Wendy Zimmermann, *Employer Hiring Practices: Differential Treatment of Hispanic and Anglo Job Seekers* (Washington: Urban Institute Press, 1990).

12. Richard A. Epstein, *Forbidden Grounds: The Case against Employment Discrimination Laws* (Cambridge, Mass.: Harvard University Press, 1992), pp. 55–58.

or inner city residence."[13] For example, these interviews suggest that employers disproportionately reject blacks because they view them as low-income persons more likely to steal, products of ineffective inner-city public school systems, and members of work-averse subcultures. Also, holding other factors constant, employers tend to avoid hiring minorities in jobs emphasizing verbal and mathematical skills and academic achievement.[14]

Employer attitudes reflect sentiments in the wider population. For example, in a 1988 survey of whites, "36% stated that blacks have less ambition than whites, 17% said they were less intelligent, 21% thought they were more likely to commit crimes, and 26% felt blacks were unable to get equal work at equal pay because they lacked a work ethic."[15] And two years later, "65 percent of whites characterized blacks as lazier than whites, and 56 percent rated blacks less intelligent than whites."[16]

These employer perceptions emphasize the major unfortunate implication of statistical discrimination: Hard-working, capable blacks and other minorities often will not even be considered for employment, let alone recruited aggressively, if they are members of groups not generally highly regarded by employers. The effect on minority job seekers is similar no matter whether a given employer decision reflects blatant prejudice or statistical discrimination that employers believe is efficient and serves them well by tending to cull out job seekers with below-average ability.

In contrast to the American hiring audits, research in other countries has focused on application submissions. Two British studies found that upon receiving identical letters of application or contemporaneous inquiries to advertised jobs, employers were more likely to respond favorably to British nationals than to others, and to Caucasian rather than non-Caucasian immigrants.[17] A similar result obtained in an Australian study: Written applications from those with Anglo-Celtic last names were favored by employers over identical

13. Joleen Kirschenman and Kathryn M. Neckerman, "'We'd Love to Hire Them, But,': The Meaning of Race for Employers," pp. 203–32 in Christopher Jencks and Paul E. Peterson, eds., *The Urban Underclass* (Washington: Brookings Institution, 1991), p. 204.

14. Braddock and McPartland, "How Minorities Continue to Be Excluded," esp. table 3, p. 14, and table 4, p. 16.

15. Douglas S. Massey and Nancy A. Denton, *American Apartheid: Segregation and the Making of the Underclass* (Cambridge, Mass.: Harvard University Press, 1993), p. 95.

16. George E. Peterson and Wayne P. Vroman, "Urban Labor Markets and Economic Opportunity," chap. 1, pp. 1–29, in George E. Peterson and Wayne Vroman, eds., *Urban Labor Markets and Job Opportunity* (Washington: Urban Institute Press, 1992), p. 18. The two cited surveys should not be interpreted as reflecting a marked increase in prejudice within two years. Answers to surveys depend on many factors, including the wording of questions and the characteristics of respondents.

17. See p. 235 in Jerome Culp and Bruce H. Dunson, "Brothers of a Different Color," pp. 233–59 in Freeman and Holzer, eds., *The Black Youth Employment Crisis*.

applications from those with Greek and, even more so, Vietnamese last names. The Australian paper also notes similar favoritism for men over women in some occupations.[18]

I know of no similar studies attempting to gauge age discrimination. Given that older workers tend to have more experience than younger workers, it would be quite difficult to develop paired younger/older résumés or testers of equal qualifications. An older applicant with experience equivalent to that of a younger one would have had abnormally few years employed.

Future research may be able to compare the results of disparate international studies. The American matched pairs actually visiting work sites and being evaluated are not directly comparable with the British and Australian initial inquiries through letters and phone calls. The strength of governmental antidiscrimination enforcement as well as the attitudes of employers toward racial and ethnic minorities both affect the treatment of minorities in different countries.

In contrast to all the studies so far reported, American federal contractors subject to affirmative action requirements slightly preferred blacks over whites by responding more favorably to similar résumés to which photographs of blacks rather than whites were attached.[19]

3.2 Recruitment Discrimination

Figure 3.1 divides the hiring process into two stages: recruiting applicants from the external labor market, and extending employment offers to applicants so recruited. Employers may discriminate in neither, either, or each stage, intentionally or unintentionally.

For example, assume an employer could reasonably be expected to draw hires from a labor market that is 25 percent black.[20] An employer whose applicants and hires were each roughly 25 percent black would appear not to be discriminating against blacks.[21] An employer whose applicants were 24 percent

18. Peter A. Riach and Judith Rich, "Testing for Racial Discrimination in the Labour Market," *Cambridge Journal of Economics* 15:3 (September 1991): 239–56. The authors also summarize their own male-female applicant study.

19. Jerry M. Newman, "Discrimination in Recruitment: An Empirical Analysis," *Industrial and Labor Relations Review* 32: 1 (October 1978): 15–23. This study is criticized by Shelby J. McIntyre, Dennis J. Moberg, and Barry Z. Posner, "Comment," *Industrial and Labor Relations Review* 33: 4 (July 1980): 543–47, and their criticism is largely effectively parried by Newman in "Reply," pp. 547–50.

20. The determination of the race or sex composition of the labor market from which an employer would be expected to draw applicants and employees is one topic of subsection 4.2.1.

21. Only occasionally will the applicant pool be *exactly* 25 percent black and thus precisely mirror the wider labor market—just as only occasionally will cumulative random selection of cards from a standard fifty-two-card deck yield a given suit 25 percent of the time. However, in the case of both applicants and cards, the result should be *close* to 25 percent. Elementary statistics textbooks explain how statisticians rigorously define "close."

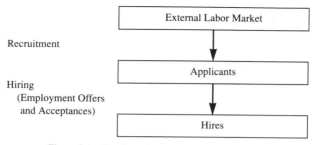

Recruitment

Hiring
(Employment Offers
and Acceptances)

Figure 3.1   The Recruitment and Hiring Processes

black, but whose hires were only 8 percent black, would have a pattern suggesting hiring discrimination, but not recruitment discrimination. One whose applicants were 9 percent black, and hires 8 percent black, would appear to be recruiting far fewer blacks than could be drawn from the labor market, but not to be discriminating in the narrow sense of hiring too few black applicants. Finally, an employer with 9 percent black applicants and 1 percent black hires would be suspect at both stages of the process. Strictly speaking, offer data, a pure representation of employer policy, should be used to assess employer behavior: Hire data reflect both employer offers and employee acceptances.

Help-wanted ads in major daily newspapers will tend to attract a representative race, ethnic, sex, and age cross-section of that presumably large segment of the population who can read or find someone to read for them; their commonality will be interest in and anticipated qualification for the advertised job. Thus, the composition of responding applicants by race, ethnicity, sex, and age would be expected to reflect—not exactly but closely—their representation in the external local labor market. The same can be said for ads in national newspapers and professional journals with respect to the national labor market.

On the other hand, targeted recruitment (considered in subsection 2.2.4) can generate applicants who are not demographically representative of the entire external labor market from which qualified and potentially interested applicants could be recruited. Thus, targeted recruitment methods can be means by which employers intentionally or unintentionally generate applicant pools in which certain subgroups of the population are largely or even totally excluded. In less extreme cases, as when targeted recruitment methods are used in conjunction with neutral methods such as major daily newspaper help-wanted ads, the representation of certain subgroups may still be significantly different from their external labor market representation. *In attracting certain groups more than others, targeted recruitment methods discriminate statistically*: The probability that potential applicants will learn of job vacancies is a function of their race, ethnicity, or other characteristics not directly related to interest in or qualification for the job at hand.

To take a concrete example: Assume 20 percent of machine operators in a metropolitan area are black. A local employer advertising a machine operator vacancy in that area's major daily newspaper would be expected to draw an applicant pool that is approximately 20 percent black. However, with targeted recruitment, an employer can easily generate a machine operator applicant pool whose representation of blacks is much higher or lower than 20 percent. By advertising a vacancy solely in newspapers or on radio stations serving the black community, or by networking with black community leaders (who can refer black job seekers to employers or suggest bulletin boards where help-wanted ads seen exclusively or predominantly by blacks could be placed), the resulting applicant pool will be predominantly, if not exclusively, black. Similarly, advertisements limited to newspapers serving white suburbs or white ethnic groups will yield a machine operator applicant pool with few, if any, blacks. Indeed, advertising only in ethnic newspapers, particularly foreign-language ones, can generate an applicant pool consisting of members of that ethnic group to the virtual exclusion of applicants of the same race but different ethnicity, let alone applicants of other races.[22]

Word-of-mouth recruitment generally will produce an applicant pool that replicates the current work force's racial and ethnic composition. Given housing and other societal segregation,[23] most people's friends, relatives, neighbors, and acquaintances are likely to be the same race, if not the same ethnic group, as they are. Word-of-mouth recruitment is much more likely to exclude applicants of certain race or ethnic groups than to exclude potential applicants by sex, age, or any other characteristics on the basis of which communities are generally not segregated. Job opportunities discussed at family gatherings, after religious services, or on the street will tend to exclude people without, but not within, a community.

It is easy to see how a small establishment can be racially, even ethnically, homogeneous. The firm perhaps starts with a few family members or close friends, all of the same ethnic group. In a small establishment, the need for additional employees is minimal and can be satisfied exclusively through personal referrals, which, because of the ethnic stratification of social networks, yield applicants—and hires—from the same ethnic group. As the firm grows, the need for new hires increases, but the larger work force, and perhaps an expanding number of customers and business associates, provides a network sufficiently extensive to generate the required number of applicants, most or all of whom are referred by and are themselves members of the owners' ethnic group.

When ethnic neighborhoods are close to an establishment, employers have

22. Employer control of the ethnic composition of the applicant pool presumes the presence of sufficient numbers of qualified and interested individuals of various ethnic groups in the geographic area from which applicants might apply. Some geographic areas are not ethnically heterogeneous, and some jobs can be filled by very few people.

23. The fundamental argument of Massey and Denton, *American Apartheid,* is that racial segregation is the key factor responsible for the perpetuation of black poverty and the creation of the urban underclass.

Table 3.1   Entrepreneurship and Unemployment

Group	Employees of own corporation (%)	Unemployment rate (%)
1980		
Asian/Pacific Islander	2.45	4.73
White	2.34	5.78
Total work force	2.12	6.51
Spanish origin	1.10	8.94
American Indian, Eskimo, and Aleut	0.94	13.15
Black	0.48	11.80
1970		
Total work force	1.48	4.37
Persons of Spanish heritage	0.85	6.62
Negro	0.43	6.96

Sources: *1980 Census of the Population, General Social and Economic Characteristics*, U.S. Summary, tables 103, 124, and 134, and *Detailed Population Characteristics*, U.S. Summary, table 279; *1970 Census of the Population, Occupational Characteristics*, tables 43 and 44, and *General Social and Economic Characteristics*, table 90. White employees of own corporation not published in 1970.

yet another incentive to hire ethnic workers: avoiding higher wages needed to attract distant workers. As noted in section 2.1, other things being equal, a worker will require a higher rate of pay to commute a longer distance, and recruiting locally allows employers to avoid paying this compensating "commuting premium." Additionally, workers living far away are often presumed to be likely to quit, be absent, or be tardy (see subsection 2.2.1).

When firms grow to a size where recruitment beyond personal referrals is necessary, they may consciously or inadvertently seek to replicate the racial or ethnic composition of their current employees on explicit or implicit grounds that employee cooperation, and therefore productivity, will be greater with an ethnically homogeneous work force. Employers thus recruit by advertising job vacancies with religious, fraternal, or community organizations to which their employees or individuals ethnically similar to them are likely to belong, or by placing ads in ethnic or community newspapers targeting the same groups. If an industry arises consisting of many small firms with similar histories and ethnically similar founders, even movement from one industry firm to another as well as advertisements in that industry's trade or union publications will reinforce the maintenance of ethnically homogeneous work forces. Members of other ethnic groups may believe that only insiders will be considered for jobs in this industry and therefore may not even bother to apply. Attorneys and human resources officials denote as *chilling* this lack of applications by members of certain groups on the basis of employer reputation.

Word-of-mouth recruitment in conjunction with racial and ethnic segregation thus implies an advantage for those who are members of ethnic groups with relatively many entrepreneurs. Indeed, table 3.1 demonstrates an almost perfect negative rank correlation between group entrepreneurship and unemployment rates.[24] Male and female unemployment rates within each group are very close to each other; women have slightly higher unemployment rates than men for Asians and Hispanics, slightly lower rates for the other groups.

Because table 3.1 reports unemployment rates on only two dates, a comparison between which is sensitive to economic conditions in those years, tables 3.2 and 3.3 are also presented, comparing black and white unemployment rates each year from 1964 to 1992 for those age sixteen and over and those age twenty and over. Table 3.3 excludes teenagers, whose labor force participation and unemployment are especially sensitive to such factors as school attendance and the availability of part-time employment. The data before and after 1972 are not directly comparable, because prior to 1972, black unemployment rates were not commonly tabulated and were presented only as an aggregate with those of other nonwhites.

Tables 3.2 and 3.3 indicate a roughly constant black-white unemployment rate ratio for three decades with, if anything, expanding differentials over time. Because whites generally have more years of education than blacks,[25] and because it is usually easier for those with more training to find work, it would not be surprising to observe somewhat higher unemployment rates for blacks even with no recruitment or hiring discrimination.

Relative black-white unemployment rates can be expressed as ratios as in tables 3.2 and 3.3 or as differences: For instance, table 3.2's 1992 15.2 percent and 6.9 percent unemployment rates for black and white men can be repre-

24. These data provide an excellent example of how small samples can yield highly statistically significant results. In the 1980 data, with five ethnic groups, there are 120 possible ways the ranks of unemployment rates and entrepreneurship can be associated. If the black and Indian unemployment rates were reversed, the data would represent the most extreme possible negative rank correlation. The probability of observing such an extreme negative result is 1/120, less than 1 percent. The actual data represent one of the four next most extreme negative results (because they require only one switch between two adjacent groups to produce a perfect negative rank correlation). Thus, the probability of observing a correlation as negative as or more negative than that in table 3.1 is 5/120 or 4.2 percent. Because there are symmetrical corresponding extreme positive associations between unemployment and entrepreneurship rates, the probability of observing a result as extreme as that in table 3.1 in either direction is 8.4 percent. Using a 5 percent level of significance, the pattern in table 3.1 would be considered significant only using a one-tailed test, but not with the more common two-tailed test. The result for 1970 is the most extreme of only six possible combinations, and since 1/6, or 16.7 percent, is greater than 5 percent, it would not be significant even at the 5 percent level. It would be improper to consider the combined entries for 1970 and 1980 as independent observations, because some of the same people are in each sample, and they are presumably affected by similar factors across the years. Similar data for 1990 were not available at the time of this writing.

25. Focusing only on those age twenty-five and older, whose high school and college education is likely to be completed, in 1980, 68.8 percent of whites and 51.2 percent of blacks were high school graduates, and 17.1 percent of whites and 8.4 percent of blacks were college graduates. See U.S. Department of Commerce, Bureau of the Census, *1980 Census of the Population*, Detailed Population Characteristics, U.S. Summary, table 262.

Table 3.2   Unemployment Rates by Race: Age Sixteen and Over

| | Unemployment rates (%) | | | | | |
| | Males | | | Females | | |
Year	White	Black and other	Ratio	White	Black and other	Ratio
1964	4.1	8.9	2.2	5.5	10.7	1.9
1965	3.6	7.4	2.1	5.0	9.2	1.8
1966	2.8	6.3	2.3	4.3	8.7	2.0
1967	2.7	6.0	2.2	4.6	9.1	2.0
1968	2.6	5.6	2.2	4.3	8.3	1.9
1969	2.5	5.3	2.1	4.2	7.8	1.9
1970	4.0	7.3	1.8	5.4	9.3	1.7
1971	4.9	9.1	1.9	6.3	10.9	1.7
1972	4.5	8.9	2.0	5.9	11.4	1.9
	White	Black	Ratio	White	Black	Ratio
1972	4.5	9.3	2.1	5.9	11.8	2.0
1973	3.8	8.0	2.1	5.3	11.1	2.1
1974	4.4	9.8	2.2	6.1	11.3	1.9
1975	7.2	14.8	2.1	8.6	14.8	1.7
1976	6.4	13.7	2.1	7.9	14.3	1.8
1977	5.5	13.3	2.4	7.3	14.9	2.0
1978	4.6	11.8	2.6	6.2	13.8	2.2
1979	4.5	11.4	2.5	5.9	13.3	2.3
1980	6.1	14.5	2.4	6.5	14.0	2.2
1981	6.5	15.7	2.4	6.9	15.6	2.3
1982	8.8	20.1	2.3	8.3	17.6	2.1
1983	8.8	20.3	2.3	7.9	18.6	2.4
1984	6.4	16.4	2.6	6.5	15.4	2.4
1985	6.1	15.3	2.5	6.4	14.9	2.3
1986	6.0	14.8	2.5	6.1	14.2	2.3
1987	5.4	12.7	2.4	5.2	13.2	2.5
1988	4.7	11.7	2.5	4.7	11.7	2.5
1989	4.5	11.5	2.6	4.5	11.4	2.5
1990	4.8	11.8	2.5	4.6	10.8	2.3
1991	6.4	12.9	2.0	5.5	11.9	2.2
1992	6.9	15.2	2.2	6.0	13.0	2.2

Source: *Economic Report of the President, 1993*, table B-38.

sented as a 2.2 ratio or an 8.3 percent difference. For males, black-white ratios are insensitive to changes in the aggregate civilian unemployment rate, but have increased over time, although not significantly, holding aggregate unemployment constant. On the other hand, black-white gaps widen when aggregate unemployment rises, and, holding aggregate unemployment constant, have grown over time. These effects are highly statistically significant. The relative female ratios and gaps have similar responses to aggregate unemployment as do those for males, but, holding aggregate unemployment constant, both ratios

Table 3.3   Unemployment Rates by Race: Age Twenty and Over

| | Unemployment rates (%) | | | | | |
| | Males | | | Females | | |
Year	White	Black and other	Ratio	White	Black and other	Ratio
1964	3.4	7.7	2.3	4.6	9.0	2.0
1965	2.9	6.0	2.1	4.0	7.5	1.9
1966	2.2	4.9	2.2	3.3	6.6	2.0
1967	2.1	4.3	2.0	3.8	7.1	1.9
1968	2.0	3.9	2.0	3.4	6.3	1.9
1969	1.9	3.7	1.9	3.4	5.8	1.7
1970	3.2	5.6	1.8	4.4	6.9	1.6
1971	4.0	7.3	1.8	5.3	8.7	1.6
1972	3.6	6.9	1.9	4.9	8.8	1.8
	White	Black	Ratio	White	Black	Ratio
1972	3.6	7.0	1.9	4.9	9.0	1.8
1973	3.0	6.0	2.0	4.3	8.6	2.0
1974	3.5	7.4	2.1	5.1	8.8	1.7
1975	6.2	12.5	2.0	7.5	12.2	1.6
1976	5.4	11.4	2.1	6.8	11.7	1.7
1977	4.7	10.7	2.3	6.2	12.3	2.0
1978	3.7	9.3	2.5	5.2	11.2	2.2
1979	3.6	9.3	2.6	5.0	10.9	2.2
1980	5.3	12.4	2.3	5.6	11.9	2.1
1981	5.6	13.5	2.4	5.9	13.4	2.3
1982	7.8	17.8	2.3	7.3	15.4	2.1
1983	7.9	18.1	2.3	6.9	16.5	2.4
1984	5.7	14.3	2.5	5.8	13.5	2.3
1985	5.4	13.2	2.4	5.7	13.1	2.3
1986	5.3	12.9	2.4	5.4	12.4	2.3
1987	4.8	11.1	2.3	4.6	11.6	2.5
1988	4.1	10.1	2.5	4.1	10.4	2.5
1989	3.9	10.0	2.6	4.0	9.8	2.5
1990	4.3	10.4	2.4	4.1	9.6	2.3
1991	5.7	11.5	2.0	4.9	10.5	2.1
1992	6.3	13.4	2.1	5.4	11.7	2.2

Source: *Economic Report of the President, 1993*, table B-38.

and the gap for those twenty and older have increased significantly over time. The gap for those sixteen and older has expanded over time, holding aggregate unemployment constant, but the effect is not statistically significant.[26]

An alternative measure of employment, the employment-population ratio, which measures the proportion of the civilian population employed, also does

26. These results are based on ordinary least squares regression equations with twenty-one annual observations (1972–92), with data taken from *Economic Report of the President* (Washington: Government Printing Office, 1993), table B-38. The statistically significant results reported in the text had t-statistics above three, and those noted as not significant had t-statistics below two.

not show relative improvement for blacks over time. White male employment-population ratios for those sixteen and older were 1.2 times black male employment-population ratios in every year from 1972 to 1992, except for 1.1 in 1972 and 1973, and 1.3 in 1982 and 1983. The ratio of the white male employment-population ratio to the black male employment-population ratio for those twenty and older was 1.1 in 1972–80 and 1986–91, and 1.2 in 1981–85 and 1992. The white female employment-population ratio increased sharply relative to that for blacks in this period, which featured dramatic growth in white female labor force participation.[27]

An advantage of the employment-population ratio over the unemployment rate is the former's inclusion and latter's exclusion of discouraged workers, those interested in working but too pessimistic about job prospects to seek employment. In the United States, unemployed persons comprise only those who have looked for a job in the last four weeks, and the labor force, on which the unemployment rate is based, consists only of the unemployed so defined and employed persons. A disadvantage of the employment-population ratio is its subsumption of students, retired persons, and others with no interest in working, a limitation that can be circumvented by focusing on nonstudent working-age individuals. Two such measures demonstrate deteriorating relative labor market status for blacks. The employment-population ratio for young black males fell relative to that of young white males between 1973 and 1989, with the relative decline especially steep for black high school dropouts.[28] And the proportions of middle-aged black males working at least one week in the preceding year and participating in the labor force decreased relative to those of white males between 1970 and 1980.[29]

Entrepreneurship is measured here by those who are employees of their own corporation rather than by those who are proprietors or partners, because the former are presumably much more likely than the latter to hire people beyond their immediate families.[30] Furthermore, only relatively small corporations would be described as an employee's own, and these small firms tend to recruit employees via word of mouth. It is of course possible that some corporations are one-person or family businesses, while sole proprietorships and partnerships may have many employees. Indeed, table 3.1's imperfect measure of entrepreneurship tells us nothing about the number of employees of

27. See ibid., table B-36.

28. John Bound and Richard B. Freeman, "What Went Wrong? The Erosion of Relative Earnings and Employment among Young Black Men in the 1980s," *Quarterly Journal of Economics* 107: 1 (February 1992): 201–32, esp. 206–8 and 210. Their samples exclude those who report no major activity other than attending school.

29. See tables 22 and 24, p. 548 and p. 550, in James P. Smith and Finis R. Welch, "Black Economic Progress after Myrdal," *Journal of Economic Literature* 27: 2 (June 1989): 519–64.

30. Rankings of alternative measures of entrepreneurship including various categories of self-employed persons were similar to those of table 3.1, with occasional reversals between whites and Asians, and Hispanics and American Indians. See 1980 sources, table 3.1.

these corporations. In any event, the relatively low success rate of blacks and other minorities in finding jobs through personal referrals (see section 2.5) is consistent with these groups' relatively low rate of entrepreneurship as defined in table 3.1.

Because correlation does not imply causality, the inference that levels of group entrepreneurship induce corresponding employment rates is not the only possible interpretation of table 3.1. Other factors may affect both entrepreneurship and employment rates. Would, for example, certain groups being harder-working than others imply the correlation observed in table 3.1?

Not necessarily. The propensity to work is better measured by labor force participation rates, not unemployment rates. Only with the additional hypothesis that harder-working people search for work more intensively than others can the unemployment rate (negatively) proxy being hard-working. Even then, factors affecting unemployment beyond job seekers' control would be ignored.

More important, each group represented in table 3.1 is heterogeneous, with separate networks even in the same geographic area. Asians', Hispanics', and whites' ancestry can be traced to several countries in Asia, Latin America, Europe, and elsewhere. Native American Indians represent many tribes. Although African-Americans are predominantly descendants of Africans brought to America as slaves in the seventeenth, eighteenth, and nineteenth centuries, an increasing number of blacks are recent immigrants from various countries in Africa and the Caribbean.

Nevertheless, the 1982 U.S. Census Characteristics of Business Owners survey data for twenty-eight metropolitan areas supports the original interpretation of table 3.1. In 93.5 percent of black firms but in only 23.2 percent of white firms were more than half the employees minorities. In fact, 57.8 percent of the white firms had no minorities at all. Most tellingly, in minority neighborhoods, more than half the employees were minorities in 96.2 percent of the black firms but in only 37.6 percent of the white firms. Even in these neighborhoods, 32.9 percent of the white firms had no minority employees. And in nonminority areas, 86.7 percent of black firms and 20.4 percent of white firms had predominantly minority work forces, and 62.7 percent of the white firms had no minorities.[31] Immigrants, who have especially high self-employment rates and tend to hire within their communities, are apparently considerably less likely than native-born whites to hire native-born blacks.[32]

Variation among entrepreneurship rates within the same ethnic group across locations or time allows examination of the proposition that entrepreneurship

31. See table 7.10, p. 271, in Timothy Bates and Constance R. Dunham, "Facilitating Upward Mobility through Small Business Ownership," chap. 7, pp. 239–81, in Peterson and Vroman, eds., *Urban Labor Markets and Job Opportunity.*

32. See pp. 394–95 in Roger Waldinger, "Changing Ladders and Musical Chairs: Ethnicity and Opportunity in Post-industrial New York," *Politics and Society* 15: 4 (1986–87): 369–401.

reduces unemployment rates within the entrepreneur's ethnic group. Ironically, desegregation in the South eroded the position of some black businesses previously protected by state-mandated segregation. Contemporaneous observers of the early desegregation period noted that "most of the hotels and restaurants which previously catered to Negroes have encountered hard times, and many have actually closed their doors."[33] Thus, when the Civil Rights Act of 1964 repealed laws prohibiting blacks from patronizing white establishments, some black businesses relying on black customers failed and, in doing so, constricted the personal networks through which black job seekers had access to work opportunities.

Although word-of-mouth recruitment will tend to operate to the disadvantage of members of minority groups not well represented among small business owners, it is of course possible that a minority worker might be hired through an advertisement in the major metropolitan daily, a help-wanted sign, or any other recruitment method, including a personal referral from a member of another ethnic group. This minority employee's personal referral network may then generate a large number of additional minority workers, even a predominantly minority work force, of a nonminority employer. However, given ethnically stratified social networks and initial recruitment within them, the dominant tendency will be for small business owners and their employees to be somewhat ethnically homogeneous. Thus, word-of-mouth recruitment, like targeted recruitment, will often discriminate against excluded groups in the statistical sense defined earlier in this section.

A special case of word-of-mouth recruitment is that of family members finding jobs for each other—either directly in the same workplace or indirectly elsewhere through a chain of referrals. In one study, the employment status of siblings (although not that of parents) had a significant effect on youth employment.[34] It is of course possible that this correlation reflects commonality in work ethic and behavior across family members rather than personal contacts.

3.3 Applicant Screening

Even when minorities discover job vacancies, are able to submit applications, and face no direct employer discrimination, they often will be less likely than

33. Andrew F. Brimmer and Henry S. Terrell, "The Economic Potential of Black Capitalism," pp. 239–56 in Harold M. Hochman, ed., *The Urban Economy* (New York: Norton, 1976), p. 241. (Originally published in *Public Policy* 19: 2 [Spring 1971]: 290–308.)

34. Albert Rees and Wayne Gray, "Family Effects in Youth Unemployment," pp. 453–64 in Richard B. Freeman and David B. Wise, eds., *The Youth Labor Market: Its Nature, Causes, and Consequences* (Chicago: University of Chicago Press, 1982). The study did not consider the detailed occupation and industry of youths, their parents, and siblings, factors that presumably affect the ability of individuals to help their family members find jobs.

whites to be considered as qualified applicants.[35] Employers initially dismiss applicants from further consideration on the basis of characteristics that tend to exclude black and other minority job seekers disproportionately.[36]

First, minorities will tend to submit inapt and incomplete application forms when they do not understand certain inquiries because of difficulties in English resulting from primary use of another language or a nonstandard English dialect, or poor education. Language difficulties are also reflected in poor diction, grammatical errors, and misspellings, all of which decrease the appeal of submitted applications, particularly when reading and writing skills are required for the job.

Second, minorities may discover and respond to job announcements more slowly than whites. If a job vacancy is both advertised in the major area daily newspaper, and known in advance by current employees, then applicants will be referred by both the newspaper ad and word of mouth. If most or all of the current employees are white, their word-of-mouth networks will tend to reach mainly other whites, who will be able to respond early, perhaps by submitting applications on the morning the ad appears in the newspaper. Because minorities will be able to respond only later after reading the ad, whites may appear to have more interest or initiative. Furthermore, if the number of applications is sufficiently large, employers may process only those submitted earliest, thus potentially freezing out minority applicants. Employers' uncertainty about the quantity and quality of future applicants also favors those who apply earlier (see section 2.4).

Minorities will also respond more slowly if they live farther from work sites than whites, a situation obtaining in particular for inner-city blacks and Hispanics facing increasing suburbanization of employment (discussed in chapter 7). They will not as quickly discover vacancy announcements in windows, or ads on bulletin boards near employers or in local newspapers serving that area. And, by living farther away, they may not be able to respond as quickly, perhaps having to mail completed applications instead of submitting them in person. Living far from the work site itself is a third disadvantage because some employers believe that employees who live far away from work are likely to be absent and tardy, and apt to quit upon finding a job nearer their homes.

A fourth problem is higher minority unemployment rates. Not only does

35. The discussion in this section is limited to *initial* applicant evaluation and does not address issues of employee testing, for which see, for example, Linda S. Gottfredson and James C. Sharf, eds., *Fairness in Employment Testing: A Special Issue of the Journal of Vocational Behavior,* vol. 33, no. 3 (December 1988).

36. Analogies to employee screening abound outside the labor market. For example, in college admissions, alumni preferences replicate the ethnicity of classes of yesteryear, while geographic distribution requirements have tended to have adverse impact on ethnic groups disproportionately residing in cities, especially Jews. See Alan M. Dershowitz, *Chutzpah* (Boston: Little, Brown, 1991), chap. 3.

time out of work yield no employer references, but it can also be interpreted as reflecting erratic work histories that render applicants poor candidates for long-term positions.[37]

The references minority applicants offer represent a fifth disadvantage; they are more likely to be minority group members whom white employers are less likely to know and may be uncomfortable contacting for reasons ranging from expected communication difficulties (interpreted broadly to include nuances of language) to uncertainty about the references' evaluation criteria. Lack of proper references—including listing friends rather than teachers or former employers—was detrimental to job-seeking Newark, New Jersey, high school seniors and recent graduates, particularly blacks, as whites more often had personal networks through which to find jobs not requiring references.[38]

Sixth, young black males in particular have relatively high rates of criminal conviction.[39] Employers may cull out applicants with criminal records, even if the applicants have been completely rehabilitated, or the crime was a one-time youthful indiscretion that will not be repeated. Because men commit far more crimes than women, consideration of convictions gives an advantage to women over men within the same ethnic group. And minority women provide a second advantage to firms whose race and sex composition is subject to regulatory scrutiny: they count in tabulations of both women and minorities.

A recent study on discrimination in mortgage lending suggests that marginal white applicants fare better than similar minorities because loan officers tend to go out of their way to help someone who "looks like you, or went to your school, or who lives in your neighborhood."[40] To the extent that this effect also obtains in the labor market, a final disadvantage for minority job seekers is lack of commonality with white decision-makers.

In particular cases, of course, these screens may operate to the disadvantage of individual whites, just as young blacks whose relatives are entrepreneurs will have unusually fruitful job referral networks. Nonetheless, the above discussion indicates that common practices often work against minority applicants. These factors tend not to affect as strongly female and older job seekers, for whom a more serious problem in applying for jobs is statistical hiring discrimination (section 3.1).

---

37. Time out of work adversely affects teenagers' employment prospects the following year, and depresses wages even years later. Male teenagers are studied by David Ellwood, "Teenage Unemployment: Permanent Scars or Temporary Blemishes," and female teenagers by Mary Corcoran, "The Employment and Wage Consequences of Teenage Women's Nonemployment," respectively, pp. 349–85 and 391–423 in Freeman and Wise, eds., *The Youth Labor Market*.

38. Culp and Dunson, "Brothers of a Different Color."

39. See "Crime and the Administration of Criminal Justice," chap. 9, pp. 451–507, in Gerald David Jaynes and Robin M. Williams, Jr., eds., *A Common Destiny: Blacks and American Society* (Washington: National Academy Press, 1989).

40. Paulette Thomas, "Boston Fed Finds Racial Discrimination in Mortgage Lending Is Still Widespread," *Wall Street Journal,* October 9, 1992, p. A3.

CHAPTER FOUR

Employment Discrimination Law

S ome legal systems allow employers to discriminate or not as they prefer, while others prohibit or compel discrimination, especially segregation. The Civil Rights Act of 1964, a landmark in American law, outlawed southern racial segregation, and promulgated, within its Title VII, a federal policy of nondiscrimination in employment. Today, even some practices that inadvertently adversely affect minority, female, and older employees and job seekers are forbidden. The complex corpus of employment discrimination law in the United States is outlined in section 4.1.[1]

Statistical and economic analysis of recruitment and hiring practices, the topic of section 4.2, is a familiar feature of American employment discrimination lawsuits. It often includes a determination of availability, i.e., the race and sex composition of the labor market from which an employer would be expected to draw applicants and employees. Subsection 4.2.3 reviews a recent federal case that provides an excellent illustration of the interaction between statistics and the law. Finally, section 4.3 discusses the concept and practice of affirmative action, with particular attention given to the regulations to which federal contractors are subject.

4.1 Employment Discrimination Law in the United States

4.1.1 Title VII of the Civil Rights Act

Title VII of the Civil Rights Act of 1964 (as amended)[2] is the most comprehensive employment discrimination statute in the United States. It prohibits

---

1. For a comprehensive discussion of these laws, see Barbara Lindemann Schlei and Paul Grossman, *Employment Discrimination Law,* 2d ed. (Washington: Bureau of National Affairs, 1983) (treatise); and Mack A. Player, Elaine W. Shoben, and Risa L. Lieberwitz, *Employment Discrimination Law: Cases and Materials* (St. Paul: West Publishing Co., 1990) (case book).

2. The Civil Rights Act of 1964, Public Law 88-352, was signed July 2, 1964, and became effective July 2, 1965.

employment discrimination against individuals on grounds of race, color, religion, sex, or national origin by private, state, and local government employers with at least fifteen employees. Title VII also forbids employment discrimination by labor unions and employment agencies of any size, and by the executive branch of the federal government.

Individual discrimination complaints and class action lawsuits alleging a "pattern and practice" of discrimination against individuals protected by Title VII can be brought against private employers, labor unions, and employment agencies by private plaintiffs and the U.S. Equal Employment Opportunity Commission (EEOC). Similar lawsuits against state and local governments can be filed by private plaintiffs and the U.S. Department of Justice. Only private plaintiffs can sue federal government agencies.

The Equal Employment Opportunity Act of 1972[3] and the Civil Rights Act of 1991[4] are the major amendments to Title VII. Before the 1972 act gave the EEOC power to sue employers, the agency had been limited to processing complaints, investigating charges, and attempting conciliation with employers. The EEOC had to refer cases against private employers to the Department of Justice, just as today it can only investigate discrimination allegations against state and local employers, who then can be sued by the Justice Department (and by private plaintiffs). The 1972 amendments also extended Title VII's coverage to state and local governments, educational institutions, employers of fifteen or more (the 1964 act had limited coverage to employers of twenty-five or more), and applicants for jobs with all covered employers; and added a section prohibiting discrimination against employees of federal agencies.[5]

The Civil Rights Act of 1991 was a response to several 1989 Supreme Court decisions, principally *Wards Cove Packing Co. v. Atonio.*[6] *Wards Cove* required plaintiffs both to highlight specific employer practices generating any statistical patterns adduced as evidence adverse to minorities or women and, if the defendant employer produced a legitimate business justification for the allegedly discriminatory practices, to persuade the court that alternative feasible practices were equally effective for the employer.

Thus, plaintiffs had to explain a paucity of black hires as a consequence of such practices as subjective hiring criteria that served as a pretext for racial

3. Public Law 92-261, effective March 24, 1972.

4. Public Law 102-166, effective November 21, 1991.

5. Section 701(b) of Title VII of the amended Civil Rights Act indicates the employers covered, including the fifteen-employee provision; section 703(a)(2) the coverage of applicants; and section 717 the requirements of nondiscrimination in federal government agencies. The increased role of the EEOC is stated indirectly over several sections. The increased employer coverage went into effect on March 24, 1973, a year after the date of the act. See United States Senate Subcommittee on Labor of the Committee on Labor and Public Welfare, *Legislative History of the Equal Employment Opportunity Act of 1972* (Washington: U.S. Government Printing Office, 1972).

6. 490 U.S. 642 (1989). An important precedent for *Wards Cove* was *Watson v. Fort Worth Bank & Trust,* 487 U.S. 977 (1987). See *Wards Cove,* 490 U.S. 656–61.

discrimination. If part of the racial disparity in hiring was the result of differential recruitment of blacks and nonblacks, plaintiffs had to establish that such policies as word-of-mouth recruitment or help-wanted ads in a suburban paper serving few blacks contributed to the disparity. Alternative employer practices suggested by plaintiffs might include an experience criterion for hiring and help-wanted ads in the region's major daily newspaper for recruitment.

The 1991 act removed part of plaintiff's burden under *Wards Cove*, while restoring defendant's burden to something sounding similar to that in force prior to *Wards Cove*. Now plaintiffs need present well-founded statistical disparities, but are no longer required to identify specific employer practices generating them. Faced with these disparities, employers must demonstrate that their practices are "job-related for the position in question and consistent with business necessity."[7] How courts will interpret "job-related" and "business necessity," and to what extent precedents from the pre–*Wards Cove* era will be determinative, remain to be seen.

Class action lawsuits often present statistical evidence showing that blacks, women, or members of other groups protected by Title VII ("protected classes") were relatively unlikely to be hired, promoted, et cetera, or relatively likely to be terminated, rejected for desired assignments, et cetera. Class members are identified specifically, e.g., black applicants for sales positions between April 15, 1991, and July 31, 1992; women qualified to be floor supervisors since February 1, 1993. In addition to seeking to establish that the employment practices producing any statistical disparities are job-related and serve reasonable business purposes, defendant employers may attempt to rebut plaintiff's statistical evidence directly. Decisions in Title VII lawsuits have in part defined the burdens of proof for plaintiffs and defendants: How strong and well founded must plaintiffs' statistical evidence be? How can employers faced with compelling statistical arguments justify their employment practices?

Title VII prohibits not only intentional discrimination, referred to as *disparate treatment,* but also employment practices that are apparently neutral but have *disparate impact* on protected classes. Thus, if an employer's written test or other employment requirement has a statistically significant *adverse impact* on a specific race/ethnic group or on women (i.e., they are significantly less likely to pass the test or to meet the requirement than whites or men), plaintiffs can bring a disparate impact lawsuit under Title VII even if the employer had no intention at all of discriminating. Individual hiring cases almost always involve charges of disparate treatment, while class action lawsuits alleging a pattern and practice of hiring discrimination often present disparate impact claims.

The disparate impact theory was first articulated in *Griggs v. Duke Power*

7. Section 703 (k)(1)(A)(i) of Title VII, as amended.

Co.[8] Duke Power's requirement of a test score equivalent to that of an average high school graduate disproportionately screened out black workers seeking promotion out of Duke Power's labor department. Given the statistical effect of the test score plus Duke Power's inability to establish that a high school diploma was related to job success, the Supreme Court ruled in favor of plaintiff Griggs and other black laborers who were not high school graduates and did not achieve a sufficiently high test score. Ironically, although *Griggs* established the precedent for disparate impact hiring cases, black applicants seeking first jobs at Duke Power or elsewhere were not protected by Title VII until the post-*Griggs* Equal Employment Opportunity Act of 1972, although cases charging gross exclusion of blacks from companies had been brought before that.

Word-of-mouth and targeted recruitment methods have been judged to be policies that have disparate impact on protected-class members,[9] even when these policies do not reflect disparate treatment, i.e., employer intent. On the other hand, the refusal to receive applications only from members of certain ethnic groups would clearly be an instance of disparate treatment.

Class action hiring cases are common. Particularly in the last few years, the EEOC has specifically alleged recruitment discrimination within some of its hiring discrimination charges. Recruitment discrimination allegations recognize the two-stage process noted in section 3.2: recruiting applicants from the external labor market, and extending employment offers to applicants so recruited. Complaints that applicants of certain groups, no matter how well qualified, are not likely to be offered jobs are claims of hiring discrimination; charges that the composition of the applicant pool does not reflect that of the external labor market are claims of recruitment discrimination; and allegations of a disparity between the composition of the external labor market and that of those hired—more rigorously, those offered employment, as only offers and not their acceptance are under employer control—comprise both, whether or not recruitment is explicitly recognized.

4.1.2 Other Laws and Orders

Employers with federal contracts of at least $10,000 have additional obligations. Executive Order 11246,[10] originally issued in 1965 and amended in 1967 by Executive Order 11375[11] to include women, has been administered by the U.S. Department of Labor's Office of Federal Contract Compliance

---

8. 401 U.S. 424 (1971).

9. Schlei and Grossman, *Employment Discrimination Law*, chap. 16.

10. Executive Order 11246 was signed on September 24, 1965. See 30 Federal Register 12319. The rules and regulations are contained in 41 Code of Federal Regulations 60-1, as amended.

11. 32 Federal Register 14303, October 13, 1967.

Programs (OFCCP).[12] The OFCCP requires federal contractors and subcontractors with fifty or more employees or a contract of at least $50,000 to identify "underutilization" of minorities (i.e., the aggregate of the groups other than whites presented in table 3.1) or women in any job group in which minority or female representation is below "availability." Availability benchmarks attempt to measure the representation of minorities and women among those qualified for and potentially interested in particular jobs.[13] The OFCCP obliges contractors to follow certain procedures to assess availability and underutilization in preparing their mandatory affirmative action plans (see subsection 4.3.1). Contractors are subject to lawsuits and debarment from federal contracts if the OFCCP judges them to be discriminating or not pursuing affirmative action.

Although neither Title VII nor Executive Order 11246 prohibits discrimination on the basis of age, the 1967 Age Discrimination in Employment Act (ADEA)[14] forbids employers to discriminate against those over forty. The ADEA's coverage is the same as that of Title VII, except that employers must have at least twenty, rather than fifteen, employees. Relative to Title VII, a large proportion of ADEA cases focus on involuntary terminations. Unlike Title VII cases, which were decided exclusively by judges until the 1991 amendments, ADEA plaintiffs have always been entitled to jury trials.

Plaintiffs bringing intentional race discrimination suits have had the right to trial by jury under two statutes passed during the Reconstruction era following the Civil War. Disparate treatment race discrimination suits against employers of any size can be filed against private and public parties under Section 1981 of the Civil Rights Act of 1866 and against local and state governments under Section 1983 of the Civil Rights Act of 1871. Lawsuits under these statutes often accompany Title VII claims.

Title VII, Executive Order 11246, and the ADEA are the most common regulations under which class action hiring issues have been argued. Other federal antidiscrimination laws, such as the Equal Pay Act of 1963 (an amend-

12. Originally the Department of Labor's OFCCP was known as the Office of Federal Contract Compliance (OFCC). In 1975, when the OFCC's mandate was expanded to include affirmative action programs for the disabled and Vietnam-era veterans, it was renamed the OFCCP. Monitoring federal contract compliance was originally the primary responsibility of sixteen, and later eleven, other offices within government agencies. There was a rough correspondence between the contract compliance functions of these offices and the sectors of the economy they regulated for other purposes: For example, the Department of the Treasury oversaw the contract compliance of banks, who were federal contractors by virtue of selling U.S. Savings Bonds. In 1979, these offices were consolidated into the OFCCP.

13. The adverb *potentially* is added because job seekers typically cannot assess their interest in a given job until they meet with company officials or employees.

14. The Age Discrimination in Employment Act of 1967, Public Law 90-202, became effective on June 12, 1968.

ment to the Fair Labor Standards Act of 1938), are not directed primarily at hiring. On the other hand, many states have fair employment practice statutes under which hiring discrimination lawsuits can be brought.

4.2 Disparate Impact Recruitment Allegations

The discussion in section 3.2 indicated that word-of-mouth and certain targeted recruitment practices can generate an applicant pool whose composition is markedly different from that of the external labor market of individuals qualified for and potentially interested in the jobs for which applicants are being recruited. If plaintiffs believe that these recruitment methods were utilized specifically to exclude minorities or others from the applicant pool, and thus ultimately from an employer's work force, they can allege disparate treatment. On the other hand, even if the employer was not in the least motivated by discrimination, plaintiffs can still sue on grounds of disparate impact.

The following subsections discuss statistical evidence of recruitment discrimination, business necessity arguments, and a federal case in which disparate impact recruitment discrimination allegations were at issue.

4.2.1 Statistical Disparities

A statistical argument in a "pure hiring" case, wherein no recruitment discrimination is alleged, could in principle be based on a comparison between the demographic composition of qualified applicants and that of those hired.[15] Theoretically, employment offers, which are purely employer decisions, rather than hires, which also reflect employee acceptances, should be analyzed, but in practice complete data on rejected job offers are rarely maintained. In principle, an employer could be faced with a disparity between the representation of blacks among hires and that among applicants, but no disparity between the

15. For simple comparisons between the composition of two nonoverlapping pools (e.g., hires and rejected applicants), various "two by two" methods can be used. For moderate and large samples, these include the test of two proportions (using a normal approximation to the binomial distribution) and the chi-square. A very simple exposition of these tests is in Farrell E. Bloch, *Statistics for Non-Statisticians,* 2d ed. (Washington, D.C.: Employment Policy Foundation, 1993). For small samples, the Fisher (or Fisher's) exact test (based on the hypergeometric distribution) must be used. The Fisher test can be used for all sample sizes, but its calculation is complex when samples are large. The chi-square and Fisher tests are discussed in some detail in Sidney Siegel, *Nonparametric Statistics for the Behavioral Sciences* (New York: McGraw-Hill, 1956), a classic text that has stood the test of time. "Two by two" tests are not emphasized in statistics books for economists, which focus primarily on regression analysis, a tool that allows one to study the effect of explanatory variables on a dependent variable while holding constant other explanatory variables. Regression analysis can be very useful in studying the hiring of applicants by race, sex, or age, holding constant such presumably qualifying factors as education and prior experience. An excellent elementary treatment of regression analysis with some introduction to probability and statistics is Ralph E. Beals, *Statistics for Economists* (Chicago: Rand McNally, 1972).

corresponding representations of those receiving job offers and applicants (although I know of no case where this type of evidence was crucial). Such a pattern could arise if blacks disproportionately rejected job offers (perhaps because a competing firm aggressively recruited blacks with better offers). It is also theoretically possible that unattractive (e.g., low paying) job offers could be extended to protected-class members in the hope that the offers will be rejected (although I know of no case in which this was alleged).

Applicant data ideally will be complete, or at least representative of all applicants. When some applications are missing, the remaining applications often will be demographically representative of the complete set. However, when missing applications are those submitted in response to a recruitment practice disproportionately reaching job seekers belonging to a specific ethnic group, the retained applications will then not necessarily reflect the ethnic composition of the set of all applications submitted. In any case, it should be possible to distinguish serious applicants (i.e., those who submitted proper rather than partial applications) from others, and to determine which applicants were qualified (for simple jobs) or how qualified they were (for more complex jobs).

In the United States, most state laws require recipients of unemployment insurance to provide evidence of job-seeking behavior to qualify for benefits. Cursorily filling out application forms or even signing company applicant logs may satisfy this requirement. Given that minorities tend to have higher unemployment rates than whites, and consequently are relatively heavily represented among unemployment insurance recipients, it is possible that minorities will be relatively heavily represented among these casual applicants, particularly for employers located near state unemployment offices. The hiring pattern of employers receiving these casual applications will thus look much worse statistically when compared against all, rather than only serious, applicants. Thus, it behooves employers to require applicants to submit detailed information such as employment histories before defining them as applicants. Various subsets of qualified applicants, such as those passing written, medical, or other tests, also may vary a good deal in their race, sex, and age composition.

Similarly, as the applicant evaluation process proceeds, some candidates will drop out of consideration because of employer rejection, applicant lack of interest upon learning more about the job, applicant receipt and acceptance of offers from other employers, or, in the case of employed job seekers, changes favorable to them at their present workplace. The demographic composition of applicants may therefore change as steps in the evaluation process are completed. For some purposes, such as analyzing the possible disparate impact of a particular employer test or requirement, it may be important to analyze the composition of the applicants eliminated and remaining at an intermediate stage of evaluation.

When applicant data are incomplete (a common situation is employer retention of application forms only for those hired and *recently* rejected), biased by employer recruitment practices, or otherwise deficient, the demographic composition of applicants may not provide suitable benchmarks against which to judge the demographic composition of those hired (or extended job offers). In these cases the benchmark against which the representation of members of various protected classes is compared is based on published data, usually the United States Census of Population ("Census"), the preeminent source of detailed information on the demographics of the American labor force.

The Census is tabulated and published decennially by the Bureau of the Census in the U.S. Department of Commerce. More timely but less detailed data are also available from the Census Bureau and from the Bureau of Labor Statistics in the U.S. Department of Labor. Some trade associations have race, sex, and national origin information about those working in the occupations they represent. Many state and local governments publish occupational and demographic data as frequently as annually; however, their occupation counts are usually simple extrapolations from the most recent Census based on an up-to-date population or gross labor force count. Thus, if there were 300 clericals in a county at the time of the last Census, and if the county population or labor force had since increased by 10 percent, local government documents might report a 10 percent increase to 330 clericals, even though no count of clericals had been undertaken.

From the Census, one can determine the representation of women; blacks; American Indians, Eskimos, and Aleuts; Asians and Pacific Islanders; and Hispanics in various detailed occupations within counties and cities. More information is generally available for employed persons than for labor force participants, a group comprising the employed and the unemployed (defined as those who have explicitly looked for a job in the four weeks preceding the survey date). The Census provides tables for the experienced civilian labor force, consisting of the employed and the unemployed who have held a job in the last five years, with the last job held defining the occupation for these experienced unemployed. Job seekers new to the labor market or returning thereto after more than a five-year absence would not be counted among the experienced unemployed and the experienced labor force. Detailed Census occupation tabulations include only those in the civilian labor force and exclude those serving in the military. Less detailed occupational data are available mostly in cities by census tracts, socioeconomically homogeneous areas corresponding to neighborhoods of roughly four thousand inhabitants.[16] Although in most cases, Census geography refers to employee residences rather than workplaces,

16. *A Researcher's Guide to the 1980 Census* (Ithaca, N.Y.: American Demographics, 1981), p. 18.

examination of commuting patterns allows analysts to develop estimates of availability at a given work site.

Availability can be considered as a rough approximation of the economic concept of labor supply. Ideally, one would like to discover how many people are qualified for and willing to work at a given job, taking into account the job's specific location, pay, hours, and all other terms and conditions of employment. A labor supply schedule indicates the amount of labor offered at various pay levels; separate labor supply schedules by race and sex then allow calculation of the race and sex composition of labor supplied at any given rate of pay, proportions that would shift over time with changes in such labor market characteristics as the number unemployed, and the pay and satisfaction of alternative job prospects, including those currently held.

Because surveying those qualified for and potentially interested in a particular job would be exceedingly time-consuming and expensive, in practice availability percentages are developed from Census and other published data sources. If the Census tables report that 20 percent of the secretaries in an employer's commuting area are black, 20 percent is used as black availability for that employer's secretarial jobs, even though it is possible that a higher or lower representation of blacks might be qualified for and interested in any particular secretarial position. Social scientists commonly use Census data as a proxy for data that would not be feasible to collect.

Applying an availability percentage based on Census data as a benchmark for a specific employer presumes that, given universal knowledge of a job opportunity, the race-sex composition of an employer's applicants should reflect that of the external labor market. Thus, if 10,000 secretaries including 2,000 blacks live within commuting distance of a secretarial job, roughly 20 percent (2,000/10,000) of the applicants for that job would be expected to be black. It is not necessary that these ten thousand secretaries be active candidates. The overwhelming majority of them will be sufficiently satisfied in their present jobs and not looking for work. Even those searching for jobs may not be aware of any specific secretarial job vacancy. Moreover, the secretaries counted at the time of the Census data collection will only partially overlap with those in the labor force at the time applications are being solicited. Indeed, only 100— 1 percent of the 10,000 secretaries in the entire labor market—may be applicants for the specific job at issue. The crucial presumption that 20 of these are expected to be black rests on the proposition that the cumulative effect of the factors just discussed should not differentially affect blacks and nonblacks. Equivalently, given universal knowledge of the job vacancy, these factors would not tend to exclude blacks more than others. The assumption of universal knowledge of the job vacancy rules out basing availability percentages on the composition of applicant pools generated by targeted recruitment policies that disproportionately inform job seekers of specific ethnic groups.

Census data for given occupations do not differentiate various characteristics of jobs. Consequently, one cannot determine different black availability percentages for assembler jobs in quiet plants and in noisy plants. As a result, use of Census data presumes that job characteristics do not disproportionately discourage members of certain groups. Thus, the proportion of black job seekers who would reject a job because of a high level of plant noise is assumed to be identical with the proportion of nonblacks who would reject the same job for the same reason.

Indeed, no published data exactly mirror any specific job: The jobs subsumed in Census or other occupational categories vary by pay scale, promotion opportunities, fringe benefits, and other terms and conditions of employment. Moreover, data published for cities and counties rarely represent the irregular areas from which employees commute. The trade-off inherent in using more precise geographic data that can more accurately reflect commuting patterns—such as that for census tracts—is further aggregation of occupational categories within them. Finally, much of the occupational data are based on answers to long-form surveys sent to roughly one in six households, and the Census Bureau's extrapolation of these data to the full population involves some sampling error.

Although practitioners are used to working with imperfect occupational and geographic data, finders of fact appreciate to varying degrees that the standards of laboratory experiments are inapposite for labor market analysis. Defendant attorneys often argue that the inevitable imprecision inherent in the use of Census data renders them too flawed to be taken seriously, a conclusion most social scientists would strongly reject.

In response to these imperfections, analysts often develop a range of availability estimates based on alternative reasonable assumptions. One can have great confidence in the analysis when the top and bottom of the availability range yield the same conclusion that the race or sex composition of hires does or does not reflect that of the external labor market from which applicants, and ultimately employees, would be expected to be drawn.

Availability percentages have an occupational and a geographic dimension. For example, in focusing on a job involving loading and removing material from a machine, availability calculations might be based on data only on "machine feeders and offbearers," the larger category of "freight, stock, and material handlers," the still broader category of "handlers, equipment cleaners, helpers, and laborers," or the much larger group of "operators, fabricators, and laborers." Each of these will yield at least slightly different availability percentages even within the same geographic area. The narrower categories may exclude individuals qualified for and interested in a given employer's jobs, while the broader categories may include individuals not qualified for or not conceivably interested in a particular job. There is no job for which all labor force participants would be qualified and in which all would be interested. Many jobs require skills and experience that most do not possess; at the other extreme, jobs that can be performed easily will pay less than the salaries many workers can command. Thus, availability calculations should not be so broadly based as to include many persons neither qualified nor interested in the jobs at issue: In the machine feeder example, data on schoolteachers or X-ray technicians should not be included in the availability calculations even upon finding an occasional schoolteacher or X-ray technician among applicants for a machine feeder and offbearer job.

Geographic areas of labor markets can be based on published commuting patterns from Census or local sources, or on residences of applicants, employees, or applicants or employees working in similar jobs in neighboring firms. The pattern of applicant residences may be affected by recruitment discrimination, and that of employee residences by both recruitment and hiring discrimination. Thus, address patterns of an employer who does not recruit blacks will falsely suggest that commuting from black neighborhoods is not feasible.

The range of availability estimates for any job will tend to understate the actual availability of minorities with high unemployment rates because the unemployed generally have a greater propensity than the employed to look for jobs. Furthermore, Census measures might understate minority availability because (1) blacks and immigrants are relatively likely to be undercounted by the Census[17] (although the extent to which undercounted people are labor force participants is unknown), and (2) as a group, minorities are younger than whites, and younger persons are more likely than older ones to be changing jobs.[18]

None of these considerations applies strongly to female availability, thus suggesting that the proportion of women among those in a given occupation is a good measure of the expected representation of women among applicants and hires for a job in that occupation. Moreover, because the geographic distribution of men and women has much less variation than that of racial and ethnic groups, availability calculations for women are not likely to be very sensitive to the use of alternative geographic areas. In contrast, different assumptions about commuting patterns from relatively black and Hispanic cities versus relatively white Anglo suburbs can have dramatic effects on black and Hispanic availability calculations.

17. See Robert Fay, Jeffrey Pasel, and Gregory Robinson, *The Coverage of the Population in the 1980 Census*, 1980 Census of Population and Housing Evaluation and Research Report PHC80-E4 (Washington: U.S. Bureau of the Census, 1988).

18. The median ages of the major population groups in 1980 were: whites, 31.3; blacks, 24.9; American Indians, Eskimos, and Aleuts, 23.4; Asians and Pacific Islanders, 28.4; and Hispanics, 23.2. See U.S. Department of Commerce, Bureau of the Census, *1980 Census of the Population, General Social and Economic Characteristics*, U.S. Summary, tables 98, 120, and 130.

Plaintiffs' attorneys sometimes argue that the extant representation of minorities and women among various occupational groups itself reflects discrimination and therefore systematically understates their availability. Accepting this point uncritically confuses several issues. First, if pre–labor market experiences such as child rearing and socialization in school have influenced, say, women to become clericals rather than craft workers, the representation of women among craft workers is clearly lower than it would be absent these influences. However, employers are given a labor market from which to hire. Are employers to be expected to retrain and to resocialize those in other occupations? Second, would not labor market discrimination—as opposed to pre–labor market factors—be expected to affect primarily unemployment and pay rather than occupational choice? And Census labor force data include the unemployed and those working at all pay levels. Finally, to the extent certain groups are excluded from various occupations, they are crowded into others (assuming they remain labor force participants). Thus, the crowding argument that availability is understated in some occupations implies that it is overstated in others, so the representation of protected classes cannot uniformly understate availability.

Indeed, any expectation that ethnic groups should be represented proportionately across occupations is naive. Even internationally, "certain occupations, certain offices or shops, became well known as the preserve of one ethnic group or another."[19] And "few, if any, societies have approximated proportional representation across sectors."[20]

Labor force data cannot furnish availability benchmarks based on age. Younger workers systematically change jobs relatively often because they are less likely than older workers to have found their niche and because they can better afford periods of unemployment if they are partially sustained by their parents or have no families to support. Moreover, older workers generally are less willing to change jobs because of insufficient time to vest fully in new jobs' retirement plans and the ability to continue building substantial pension benefits in their current, often long-term, positions. In addition, new jobs often involve specific training for which workers implicitly invest in the form of reduced compensation, reaping the returns later in their careers.[21] Older workers have a shorter time frame during which to receive these benefits in new jobs, and are already doing so in their present employ. For all these reasons, the propensity to change jobs decreases with age and renders age profiles of the employed or the labor force inappropriate availability benchmarks for older

---

19. Donald L. Horowitz, *Ethnic Groups in Conflict* (Berkeley: University of California Press, 1985), p. 111.

20. Ibid., p. 677.

21. See Gary S. Becker, *Human Capital: A Theoretical and Empirical Analysis with Special Reference to Education,* 2d ed. (Chicago: University of Chicago Press, 1975).

workers.[22] Thus, if 30 percent of computer programmers in a labor market are over forty years old, the representation of those over forty among computer programmer applicants and new hires would be expected to be considerably below 30 percent.

Nevertheless, some attorneys present Census age availability data, naively or tendentiously ignoring the arguments just presented. Others seek to justify using published age data on grounds that older workers are inhibited from job changes because of pervasive employer discrimination against them, a position supported by the concentration of age discrimination lawsuits in the area of terminations and reductions in force, and the difficulties many terminated older workers have in finding new jobs. However, the discrimination older workers face is hardly a sufficient condition for age availability benchmarks' resuscitation, which would require in addition that older workers' reduced propensity to change jobs because of anticipated discrimination just cancels the factors noted in the previous paragraph and is the responsibility of employers seeking new hires. The difficulty of measuring the anticipatory discrimination effect alone invalidates published age benchmarks.

In any case, it would appear that the discriminatory effects on the age composition of applicants are not very large. First, practices such as word-of-mouth and targeted recruitment are much more likely to affect members of minority groups than older workers. Second, lawsuits alleging recruitment and hiring discrimination by age are much less common than those alleging recruitment and hiring discrimination by race or even by sex. Third, if employers' responsibility does not include correcting applicants' pre–labor market occupational choices, it would also presumably not include changing perceptions older workers may have about the job market, and would be limited to treating older applicants and employees fairly.

In sum, Census or other published data generally can provide useful, albeit imperfect, availability benchmarks for the expected race and sex composition of hires. Analysts should construct a range of estimates to represent an array of reasonable alternatives, and each benchmark should incorporate well-founded occupational and geographic assumptions. On the other hand, analysts should eschew developing age availability measures from published employment or labor force data.

In a lawsuit alleging recruitment discrimination, the basic statistical question is whether the race and sex composition of applicants fairly reflects that of the external labor market. In contrast to hiring analyses, applicant qualifications are irrelevant, because the set of all applicants indicates whom an employer is successfully recruiting. More important is to tabulate only serious

22. At least through the 1980 Census, occupation profiles by age were not published by the Census in the same detail as occupational profiles by race and sex.

applicants: Total application counts may include casual inquiries. At any rate, because the various stages of the job candidate evaluation process do not have to be scrutinized in assessing recruitment, analysis of recruitment is simpler than that of hiring. However, because the hiring or representation of protected-class members normally draws the attention of government or private plaintiff attorneys, "pure recruitment" cases will be rare (I know of none).

What differences between benchmarks and employer outcomes will the law tolerate? If black availability is 20 percent, and an employer hires fifteen rather than the expected twenty blacks out of one hundred total hires, will there be a presumption of guilt?

Statisticians can easily calculate the probability of hiring no more than fifteen (or any other number of blacks) out of one hundred hires from a 20 percent black labor market. This calculation uses a statistical distribution known as the exact binomial, and can be approximated using a normal approximation to the binomial distribution if the number of total hires is above thirty and the expected number of hires in each group exceeds five.[23] If the probability of hiring no more than fifteen blacks is relatively high, then the hiring process would not be suspect. On the other hand, if the probability of hiring fifteen or fewer blacks is relatively small, then the proposition that the result of the hiring process is consistent with an expected black representation of 20 percent would be seriously questioned.

Students of statistics may recall that disparities between observed results (e.g., fifteen blacks hired) and expected results (i.e., twenty blacks hired, equivalently, a 20 percent representation of blacks among total hires) were generally regarded as statistically significant if the probability of observing them by chance was below 5 percent. If one is concerned about disparities where the observed value is sharply above as well as sharply below the expected value, then the normal distribution cutoff point corresponding to this 5 percent probability is a *z-score* of plus or minus 1.96, equivalently a disparity of 1.96 standard deviations. The level 1.96 is commonly approximated by a z-score of 2, or two standard deviations, beyond which is a 4.56 percent probability of occurrence in both directions: 2.28 percent above plus 2, and 2.28 percent below minus 2. The higher the z-score and the corresponding number of standard deviations, the less likely the observed result is consistent with the expected pattern.

Nothing is sacred about a significance level of 5 percent or its approximate equivalent of two standard deviations (i.e., a z-score of 2), even though it is the

23. In this example, one hundred total hires is clearly above thirty. And both the expected number of black hires (20 percent of one hundred, or twenty) and the expected number of nonblack hires (80 percent of one hundred, or eighty)—the only other group of interest in the example—are greater than five. The statistical tests used are different from those comparing the composition of applicants with that of hires, for which see note 15 above.

most widely used litmus test in a variety of applied statistical applications. Any user of statistics is free to use other probabilities and standard deviation levels. Federal courts cite a criterion of two *to three* standard deviations, with two standard deviations alone being adopted in many circuits.[24] The limitations of Census data—apart from the quantifiable imprecision due to sampling error—suggest a post hoc justification of the Supreme Court's two to three standard deviation benchmark, namely, use of a lower (stricter for employers) standard deviation criterion when company, rather than economy-wide, data underlie the comparisons. Thus, a disparity based purely on company data, such as an applicants versus hires study, might be judged against two standard deviations, while a comparison of applicants or hires versus Census data might be held to a yardstick of, say, 2.576 standard deviations, beyond which disparities will occur by chance only 1 percent of the time—one-half of 1 percent above plus 2.576, and one-half of 1 percent below minus 2.576. I do not suggest the criterion of three standard deviations because three standard deviations is not customarily used as a significance criterion in statistical research in any applied area.

Those whose initial acquaintance with statistics occurred outside the employment discrimination arena may find it odd that bottom-line statistical results in employment discrimination cases are expressed in standard deviations rather than in probabilities or confidence intervals.[25] Indeed, many statistical calculations do not involve any measure of standard deviations, even as an intermediate result. However, because of the early introduction of the two to three standard deviation criterion, the standard deviation concept holds a preeminence in employment discrimination law that it does not command elsewhere. In fact, for the convenience of courts and attorneys, the bottom lines of

24. I am not aware of a three-standard-deviation criterion being adopted by any circuit. The probability of observing a disparity of three standard deviations or more in either direction is 13/100 of 1 percent, and in both directions combined 27/100 of 1 percent, a far cry from 5 percent! The disparities in some early statistical cases were so egregious that the distinction between two and three standard deviations was not important. The two to three standard deviation criterion was introduced in a grand jury selection case, *Castaneda v. Partida,* 430 U.S. 482, 496–97 n. 17 (1977), and first applied to an employment discrimination matter in *Hazelwood School District v. United States,* 433 U.S. 299, 308–9 n. 14 (1977). Interestingly, in each of these cases, the wording of the footnotes is that *if* the disparities are equivalent to two or three standard deviations, they would be suspect, rather than the alternative wording that to be suspect the disparities *must be* equivalent to at least two to three standard deviations. If a two or three standard deviation criterion is thus sufficient, but not necessary, for suspicion, then smaller disparities might also be suspect.

25. A confidence interval indicates the probability of observing a result within a band. For example, rather than expressing the text example result of fifteen blacks hired in terms of a comparison with the twenty blacks expected to be hired, one could say that, based on observing fifteen blacks hired, there is a 95 percent chance that the employer's underlying hiring rate of blacks is between 8 and 22 percent. Because this 8 to 22 percent interval includes 20 percent, the result would be consistent with a 20 percent representation of blacks among hires.

statistical tests not involving standard deviations are often translated into a standard deviation equivalent by using the corresponding points on the standard normal distribution.

In the example posed, if black availability were 20 percent, an employer with one hundred hires would have to have twenty black hires among them to be at parity with the external labor market, but would be within two standard deviations of this expected level with twelve or more blacks, and within three standard deviations with eight or more. In particular, because fifteen exceeds twelve, fifteen black hires would be regarded as consistent with a process generating a 20 percent representation rate of blacks among total hires.[26]

Because twelve corresponds to a point two standard deviations below parity, employers hiring one hundred employees from a 20 percent black labor market without regard to race will, about 2.28 percent of the time, hire twelve or fewer blacks. In general, employers with statistically significant shortfalls of certain groups of workers will occasionally be using race-neutral recruitment and hiring policies. Thus, statistics creates the presumption but not the proof of discrimination. That presumption is of course stronger, the greater the number of standard deviations from parity.

If the total number of hires or black availability is sufficiently low, then even zero black hires will not be statistically significant. In a labor market that is 5 percent black, an employer could hire up to seventy-three whites without having a statistically significant shortfall of blacks.[27] The cumulative effect on minority job seekers of decisions by many employers, no one of whom has a statistically significant shortfall, can be powerful: If fifty firms are each hiring seventy whites and no blacks in a labor market with 5 percent black availability, no one of them will have a statistically significant shortfall because seventy is below seventy-three. Yet among 3,500 (50 times 70) hires, none will be black, even though 175 (5 percent of 3,500) would be expected to be.

The following example is representative of many statistically oriented hiring cases where applicant data cannot be used and Census data are used by both sides to provide benchmarks. Suppose during the legally relevant time period 8 percent of a firm's hires are black. Plaintiff presents a 17 to 20 percent range of black availability benchmarks, and defendant presents a corresponding range of 14 to 18 percent. Even compared against plaintiff's bottom 17 percent

26. Relative to an expected twenty black hires, fifteen would represent a shortfall of only 1.25 standard deviations, a level not considered statistically significant using any conventional criterion.

27. The probability of hiring seventy-three consecutive whites from a labor market that is 95 percent white is .95 to the 73d power, or .0236, which is above the .0228 probability corresponding to two standard deviations. However, the probability of hiring seventy-four consecutive whites is .95 to the 74th power, or .0225, below .0228 and therefore a significant result using the two-standard-deviation criterion.

benchmark, the firm's 8 percent hires are statistically significantly low, using two standard deviations or whatever statistical criterion the court prefers. However, compared against the 14 to 15 percent defendant availability range, 8 percent is no longer statistically significant. If the court accepts defendant's benchmarks, then defendant wins the case. If the court accepts plaintiff's benchmarks, then the burden shifts to defendant to provide a legitimate explanation for the statistically significant shortfall of black hires.

4.2.2 Business Necessity

Even when plaintiffs establish significant and well-founded statistical disparities, defendant employers can prevail if the disparities are the result of practices that, in the words of the Civil Rights Act of 1991, are "job-related for the position in question and consistent with business necessity." This phrase leaves much room for interpretation.

Thus, in a hiring case, if Hispanic clerk-typist applicants were rejected at a significantly higher rate than Anglo clerk-typist applicants, an employer could presumably nonetheless win a lawsuit by showing that the applicants were rejected because they failed a typing test *and* that the typing test was job-related, that is, predictive of job success.

Applicant characteristics that are job-related in one context need not be in another. Thus, although high school and college degrees may be bona fide requirements for some positions, they are not universally so. *Griggs*, discussed above, is the classic case. A striking example is *James v. Stockham Valves and Fittings Company*,[28] in which an employer of manual laborers claimed to hire whites at a significantly greater rate than blacks because of their greater years of formal education. The court, however, found education to be unrelated to the competent performance of manual labor and ruled for the black plaintiff.[29]

Word-of-mouth recruitment might be justified by a business necessity argument based on avoiding costs of placing classified help-wanted ads. Similarly, targeted recruitment could be defended on grounds that an ad in a neighborhood or suburban newspaper (with residents happening to be ethnically similar to the employer) is cheaper to place than the same ad in a large metropolitan daily.

Although the Supreme Court has not yet issued a decisive ruling on this point, it would appear that these business necessity arguments would not be considered persuasive because cost savings of avoiding newspaper ads are minimal. An argument not so far considered by the courts to be relevant is that by excluding some potential (protected class) applicants, an employer's business could actually be harmed by not allowing more competition and the re-

28. 559 F. 2d 310 (5th Cir. 1977).
29. Ibid., at 332.

sultant greater chance for an excellent match between job vacancy and applicant. This argument can of course be countered by the cost of interviewing applicants and the ease of effecting a good match in some jobs, both of which factors militate against evaluating large numbers of applicants.

Federal courts have rejected employer residency requirements that limit geographical qualifications to areas with few or no minorities, even when the employer is a municipality hiring only its own residents.[30] Courts have also carefully scrutinized employers' arguments that minorities were not hired because they live farther from the workplace than whites. In these cases, "gerrymandered" residence patterns of applicants, with whites living far from the work site being represented among applicants in much greater numbers than blacks living closer, provide strong evidence for plaintiffs.[31]

4.2.3 A Federal Case

In 1988 the EEOC sued Chicago manufacturer O&G Spring and Wire Forms Specialty Company,[32] alleging racial discrimination against blacks in violation of Title VII of the Civil Rights Act of 1964.[33] The EEOC charged that O&G discriminated against blacks in recruitment and hiring in part because its Polish immigrant owner's recruitment policy included personal referrals generated by his largely Polish immigrant work force. The case was decided prior to *Wards Cove* and reheard thereafter, and provides an excellent example of judicial analysis of recruitment discrimination.

---

30. See, for example, *Newark Branch N.A.A.C.P. v. Town of Harrison, N.J.*, 940 F. 2d 792 (3d Cir. 1991).

31. *Mister v. Illinois Central Gulf Railroad*, 832 F. 2d 1427 (7th Cir. 1987).

32. I served as plaintiff EEOC's rebuttal expert witness in this case to testify about defendant O&G's racial patterns and practices of recruitment and hiring. The EEOC and O&G also retained expert witnesses to introduce primary economic and statistical evidence for their cases in chief. Although in any given year, my retention as an expert witness may be dominated by the EEOC (who represent plaintiffs in many large statistical cases), or by defendant employers, I have done about an equal amount of work on behalf of plaintiffs and defendants. At any rate, disclosure of my participation in this case will allow readers to judge whether my appearance as a witness influences my discussion.

33. *Equal Employment Opportunity Commission v. O&G Spring and Wire Forms Specialty Company*, 705 F. Supp. 400 (N.D. Ill. 1988). Only the race discrimination arguments are discussed here. The court also heard simpler and, for present purposes, much less interesting allegations that O&G discriminated against older job seekers. It ruled that the defendant was not liable for age discrimination in large part because the published age data adduced by the EEOC were not considered to be a proper benchmark against which to judge the age composition of new hires. Furthermore, O&G employed substantial numbers of older workers. In general, the composition of employees is far less preferred than that of hires or offers in assessing hiring discrimination because many employees were hired before or after the legally relevant period, while some others hired during that period may no longer be employed.

The EEOC's case in chief was based primarily on statistics. In the seven-year period from 1979 to 1985, O&G hired eighty-seven employees to operate its kick and punch presses. None of these hires was black. Seven percent of the 1984 and 1985 application forms were submitted by blacks. The earlier applications were legally destroyed, because the EEOC's recordkeeping regulations then required employers to keep applications only for six months, and to retain them for a longer period only if a charge of discrimination had been filed.[34]

Given O&G's recruitment policies, the EEOC believed the representation of blacks among O&G's applicants to be artificially low. Accordingly, the EEOC developed several availability benchmarks against which to compare O&G's hiring of zero blacks out of eighty-seven total hires.

First, the 1980 Census representation of blacks among machine operators living within one mile of O&G's plant was approximately 23 percent. Next, according to the Employer Information Reports—usually referred to as EEO-1 reports—indicating the race and sex composition of broad occupational categories[35] within the work forces of private employers with one hundred or more employees, the representation of blacks among operatives (a large occupational category including machine operators) working for employers in O&G's zip code ranged between 26.7 percent in 1982 and 28.8 percent in 1985. Finally, the representation of blacks in the broad operators, fabricators, and laborers occupational category was 35.1 percent in the entire city of Chicago, 22.5 percent in the six-county Chicago Standard Metropolitan Statistical Area ("SMSA"), and a level in between in Cook County, which includes Chicago.

Against even the lowest 22.5 percent benchmark, O&G's zero blacks out of eighty-seven total hires was highly significant statistically. The opinion reports a probability of observing zero hires by chance at less than three in one million. This probability is based on a disparity of more than five standard deviations.[36] Obviously, the disparity would be even greater against any of the other benchmarks—all above 22.5 percent.

34. Effective August 26, 1991, the retention period for applications and other records was extended to one year. See 56 Federal Register 144, July 26, 1991.

35. Table 6.4 lists these.

36. The EEOC's expert witness used the normal approximation to the binomial distribution to obtain a shortfall of 5.02 standard deviations, a result that in fact can occur by chance only three times in *ten* million. With the same data, the precise exact binomial distribution calculation yields a bottom-line probability of less than three in ten *billion*, about a thousandth of the probability associated with a 5.02 standard deviation disparity! The reason for the difference in the two test results is that the normal distribution is a less reliable approximation to the exact binomial for extremely low probability events. Satisfaction of the standard criteria for use of the normal approximation to the binomial, at least thirty observations and an expected number of hires in each group of at least five—here 87 total hires, an expected number of blacks of 19.575 (.225 times 87), and an expected number of nonblacks of 67.425 (.775 times 87)—assures that the normal distribution will provide excellent approximations only for the vast majority of instances that do not involve extremely unlikely events.

Most interestingly, after the EEOC's charge was filed, O&G hired five blacks among its twelve 1986 and 1987 operative hires, a striking difference from zero blacks out of eighty-seven hires for the same jobs in the prior seven years. This is but one of several instances I have observed where an employer's record in hiring protected-class members is significantly different before and after a charge or complaint is filed. It would appear that generating different ethnic compositions of applicants is not difficult for employers, given the array of available recruitment policies, particularly targeted recruitment. In general, plaintiffs seek to convince courts that the early period with few protected-class hires reflected discrimination, and the later period neutrality, while defendants argue that the early period practices were neutral and the later period enlisted aggressive recruitment of protected-class members.

O&G responded with two defenses against the EEOC's availability argument: First, the plaintiff's benchmarks were flawed; second, even if the statistical disparity is accepted, it can be explained by legitimate business practices.

Most of defendant O&G's arguments against the EEOC's availability benchmarks were weak. O&G of course pointed out some intrinsic imperfections in the Census occupational data, in particular, the conflation of employees working at large and small plants, and using various machinery; but O&G did not present alternative availability benchmarks taking these factors into account, or even evidence that the proportion of blacks employed or seeking jobs varies by firm size or type of machinery used. O&G also suggested that the EEOC should have jettisoned the carefully collected Census data in favor of a survey designed specifically for this case, but did not itself undertake such a project.

One argument with some merit but presented only in inchoate form during the trial is based on O&G's founders and many employees being immigrants. Assume 1,000 individuals are seeking employment in the relevant labor market: 220 blacks, 50 Poles who do not speak English well enough to work for an English-speaking employer, and 730 others. If these individuals represented the entire labor market, black availability would be 22 percent (220/1,000), below even the low end of the range presented by the EEOC.

Now suppose these thousand workers can do no work but operate the machines of ten employers, each of whom has identical jobs and job vacancy rates, but only one of whom can accommodate the Polish workers. Perhaps only English is spoken in nine shops, and Polish and English in the tenth. Then assuming universal knowledge of the vacancies, and no geographic advantages of any employer vis-à-vis the residences of the thousand job-seekers, each employer would be expected to receive applications from twenty-two blacks and seventy-three nonblacks/non-Poles. Nine of the ten would receive no applications from Poles, and the tenth would receive applications from all fifty Poles. Under these assumptions, black availability for the tenth employer is 15.2 percent (22/145), and 23.2 percent (22/95) for the other nine. The assumption of universal knowledge is critical here; the exercise is to identify the proportion of blacks among applicants assuming job vacancy information is widely disseminated, not spread to only a few through word-of-mouth or targeted recruitment.

Had this argument been presented rigorously and accepted in toto, including even the strong assumption that 5 percent of the market consisted of Polish-born workers with English-language deficiencies so severe as to disqualify them for machine operator jobs with English-speaking employers, the EEOC would still have prevailed in its prima facie case because even against 15.2 percent availability, zero black hires out of a total of eighty-seven can occur by chance with probability roughly one in two million (using the exact binomial distribution).[37]

Establishing a prima facie case is not tantamount to winning a lawsuit. O&G presented two basic business necessity arguments, which, as in most cases with highly significant disparities, were, at least to labor economists, much more persuasive than their attacks on the EEOC's statistical case.

First, O&G noted that recruiting via word of mouth and accepting walk-ins obviated costs of placing newspaper ads and evaluating the respondents thereto. An implicit presumption here was that word-of-mouth recruitment plus walk-ins provided a sufficient number of new hires for O&G's work force of approximately fifty. Second, O&G emphasized the technical training Polish-born workers receive in high school. Without investigating the extent to which this training differs from that acquired elsewhere in schools or on the job, it seems very reasonable to posit that O&G's Polish owners could more easily evaluate that training than they could similar training obtained outside Poland. In the language of section 3.1, O&G's applicant evaluation costs are lower for Poles than for others, an argument supporting statistical discrimination in favor of Poles.

O&G did not emphasize efficiencies gained from word-of-mouth recruitment, including those resulting from work teams of culturally similar workers, many of whom might be able to commute together (see section 2.1). Even if these arguments were considered, prudence would dictate eschewing them, lest they be interpreted as reflecting a desire to exclude non-Poles in general and blacks in particular. And O&G did not maintain that their jobs required Polish-language competence as a condition of employment, certainly a reasonable qualification for such employers as a Polish-language newspaper. As O&G grew, only slightly more than half their hires were Polish and about 15 percent were Hispanic, seemingly demonstrating the owners' and initial employees' eventual exhaustion of their presumably largely Polish personal

37. With the normal approximation to the binomial distribution, the test used by the EEOC's primary expert, the disparity is equivalent to a less striking but still highly significant 3.95 standard deviations (equivalent to a probability of roughly one in twenty-five thousand).

network. The recruitment and hiring practices generating Hispanic employees did not also attract blacks.

The court rejected O&G's business necessity arguments because mere articulation of nondiscriminatory reasons for word-of-mouth recruitment was held to be insufficient to rebut EEOC's statistical case. Because this December 1988 opinion preceded *Wards Cove*, defendants were required at that time to provide nondiscriminatory explanations for any disparities based on statistical arguments they could not rebut. The court found O&G's arguments to provide only partial explanation for the shortfall of blacks, and apparently was particularly impressed by absolutely no black hires in 1979–85.

After the *Wards Cove* decision in July 1989, O&G filed a motion for reconsideration.[38] Under *Wards Cove*, plaintiffs were required not merely to present statistical arguments but also to identify specific employer practices responsible for the reported disparities. The defendant employer then had "to demonstrate a 'legitimate employer purpose' for the suspect employer practice and it is no longer necessary that the practice be 'essential' or 'indispensable.'"[39] In response, a plaintiff had to show "that either the employer's alleged business justification is a pretext for unlawful discrimination or that alternative practices are available that will achieve the same business ends with less racial impact."[40]

Under the *Wards Cove* criteria, the court in January 1990 found O&G's word-of-mouth recruitment policies to serve a legitimate business purpose, citing O&G's arguments at the 1988 trial. However, about two-thirds of O&G's hires were walk-ins rather than word-of-mouth recruits. And no walk-in hires were black. Thus, the court found that O&G's disparate treatment of black walk-in applicants was responsible for the disparities presented by the EEOC. The court noted that O&G could have avoided liability by hiring black walk-ins on the same basis as it hired others. Although the court maintained its earlier decision in favor of the EEOC's allegation of hiring discrimination, it reversed its 1988 finding that word-of-mouth referral policy was an instrument of recruitment discrimination.

A purely legal justification for word-of-mouth recruitment is that it does not reflect an active employer policy, but rather passive employer reliance on either recruitment by employees[41] or unsolicited inquiries by job seekers within the employer's community.[42] No economic or statistical argument can be adduced for or against this interpretation.

38. 732 F. Supp. 72 (N.D. Ill. 1990).
39. Ibid., at 73.
40. Ibid.
41. *EEOC v. Chicago Miniature Lamp Works*, 947 F. 2d 292, 305 (7th Cir. 1991).
42. *EEOC v. Consolidated Service Systems*, 989 F. 2d 233 (7th Cir. 1993). As the EEOC's expert witness in this case, I presented evidence of striking disparities between the representation of

Under the Civil Rights Act of 1991, it would appear that the court's opinion in *O&G Spring and Wire* would be more like that of December 1988 than that of January 1990. As noted in subsection 4.1.1, under the Civil Rights Act of 1991, plaintiffs need present well-founded statistical disparities, but are no longer obliged to identify specific employer practices generating them. Employers are required to show that their practices are "job-related for the position in question and consistent with business necessity," a concept that awaits judicial interpretation.

4.3 Affirmative Action

"Affirmative action" has at least three interpretations. The term was introduced in 1961 in Executive Order 10925,[43] which merely admonished employers to take affirmative action to ensure nondiscrimination. Three years later, Title VII instructed courts finding employers guilty of discrimination to "order such affirmative action as may be appropriate, which may include, but is not limited to, reinstatement or hiring of employees, with or without backpay."[44] Affirmative action was associated here with remedial efforts.

In the next year, Executive Order 11246 obliged contractors to take affirmative action to ensure that applicants are employed, and employees treated without discrimination, a definition similar to that in Executive Order 10925. However, in enforcing these requirements, the Department of Labor developed its Philadelphia Plan, aimed at increasing the representation of minorities in the construction trades, and later its Revised Order Number 4, both of which were precursors of the numerical "goals and timetables" obligations of federal contractors. Thus was affirmative action linked with numerical yardsticks and an emphasis on results rather than treatment.[45]

Some interpreted the original concept of affirmative action as a recommendation that employers extend their recruitment methods to reach out to potential applicants who would not otherwise be contacted and made aware of job vacancies. For example, rather than relying on word-of-mouth recruitment, a white employer might advertise job vacancies in the black commu-

---

Koreans in the external labor market and that among the Korean immigrant employer's applicants and hires. The Court of Appeals did not dispute my analysis, but found the disparities nonprobative of disparate treatment. Apparently in view of *Chicago Miniature*, the EEOC did not appeal the district court's finding of no disparate impact.

43. This order was issued on March 6, 1961. See 26 Federal Register 1977.

44. Section 706(g)(1).

45. For a detailed legal analysis of problems with applying racial preferences in employment, contractor set-asides, and broadcast license grants, see Marc Rosenblum, "Race-Conscious Employment Programs in the Post-Brennan Era: An End to Falsely Remedial Preferences?" *Houston Law Review* 28: 5 (October 1991): 993–1093.

nity, using one or more of the targeted recruitment methods considered in section 2.2.4. Today, federal contractors in the United States have specific affirmative action requirements beyond merely encouraging recruitment and "outreach."[46]

4.3.1 OFCCP Regulations

The Department of Labor's 1968 regulations concerning the implementation of Executive Order 11246[47] oblige federal contractors or subcontractors with fifty or more employees or a contract of at least $50,000 to identify "underutilization" of minorities or women in any job group in which minority (defined as the aggregate of the groups other than whites appearing in table 3.1, namely, blacks, Hispanics, Asians, and American Indians) or female representation is below availability. Underutilization in any job group necessitates corrective goals and timetables. Job groups are sets of roughly homogeneous jobs; most employers divide their work forces into ten or so job groups, often corresponding to broad categories such as professionals, clericals, and laborers listed on EEO-1 reports (see table 6.4).

Rather than basing its benchmarks on the availability methodology discussed in the previous section, the OFCCP uses its own ill-conceived set of "Eight Factors," well known to human resources officials in firms that are federal contractors. Two of these eight factors are reasonable; the remaining six are either redundant or improper.

In determining the acceptable representation of minorities within job groups, federal contractors must consider at least the following eight factors:[48]

1. The minority population of the labor area surrounding the facility;
2. The size of the minority unemployment force in the labor area surrounding the facility;
3. The percentage of the minority work force as compared with the total work force in the immediate labor area;
4. The general availability of minorities having requisite skills in the immediate labor area;
5. The availability of minorities having requisite skills in an area in which the contractor can reasonably recruit;
6. The availability of promotable and transferable minorities within the contractor's organization;
7. The existence of training institutions capable of training persons in the requisite skills; and

---

46. For an analysis of similar policies in other countries, see Thomas Sowell, *Preferential Policies: An International Perspective* (New York: Morrow, 1990).

47. 41 Code of Federal Regulations 60-1, issued May 28, 1968.

48. See 41 Code of Federal Regulations 60-2.

8. The degree of training which the contractor is reasonably able to undertake as a means of making all job classes available to minorities.

The eight factors for females are very similar. Factors 6, 7, and 8 are identical. Factors 1–4 for females are the same as factors 2–5 for minorities. Factor 1 for minorities is replaced by factor 5 for females:

5. The availability of women seeking employment in the labor or recruitment area of the contractor.

Factor 6 is apposite for jobs filled by promotion or transfer within an employer's organization. It asks employers to consider the representation of minorities and women among those employed who would be qualified for promotions and transfers. Factors 7 and 8 recognize that determining potentially qualified employees may involve considering the training necessary for the new position. However, unlike the other six factors, they are nonquantitative and more properly classified simply as issues affecting factor 6.[49]

Factors 1–5 refer to filling job vacancies with new hires. Minority factor 5 (equivalently, female factor 4) conforms to the availability concept discussed in the prior section and used by federal courts and the EEOC.

Given that factor 5 for minorities (factor 4 for women) corresponds to this availability concept, why include the other factors? Factor 1, based on the population, will always be irrelevant for availability because the total population includes infants, retired persons, and others who have no interest in working. Factors 2 and 3 refer to all unemployed persons and all those in the labor force, both of which groups will always be overinclusive as a source of employees because for no job will all be qualified and interested. In particular, those not qualified for skilled jobs and those qualified for but not interested in relatively low-paying unskilled jobs should be excluded from availability counts.

Factor 4 is almost the same as factor 5, the only difference being between "immediate labor area" and "area in which the contractor can reasonably recruit." When these two areas coincide, as they will for jobs in which all recruitment is local, factor 4 is redundant. When recruiting involves regional or national search, as is common for professional positions, factor 4's immediate labor area is too restrictive.

In practice, knowledgeable contractors assign negligible weights to the improper factors, essentially relying on factor 5 for jobs filled externally and factor 6 for jobs filled internally. When a job is filled via local recruitment, contractors can give equal weight to factor 5 and redundant factor 4. If the representation of minorities or women among the entire population, labor

---

49. Factor seven alternatively can be interpreted as measuring the availability of those hired directly after graduation from school or completion of a training program.

force, or the unemployed happens to be close to properly determined availability, then the weight given to factor 5 can be split among other factors. These ruses aside, the only proper interpretation of the OFCCP regulations is to use factor 5 for external hires and factor 6 for internal promotions.

Relative to the availability yardsticks, contractors must denote shortfalls of even one minority or woman among employees in a given job group as "underutilization." Thus, if minority availability for clericals is 25 percent, an employer with twenty-four minorities among one hundred clericals is "underutilizing" minority clericals. In essence, employers cannot be below average in their minority or female representation in any job group.

Again, the OFCCP's approach differs from that of the courts and the EEOC, whose strictest criterion allows employers to hire minorities and women within a two-standard-deviation band of availability. With this criterion, given one hundred clericals and 25 percent minority availability, seventeen or more minority clericals is acceptable. Moreover, the courts and the EEOC typically focus on hires within a limited time period, not on all employees. Legal considerations aside, some employees may have been hired in the past when minority and female availability was different (generally lower because of the growth over time of minority and female representation in the labor force), so that contemporary availability benchmarks will be too high. Furthermore, holding constant minority or female representation, it will be more difficult to establish a statistically significant disparity with the ordinarily smaller number of new hires than with the greater number of total employees.

Whatever one's position on affirmative action or antidiscrimination regulation, why burden federal contractors with an availability methodology that is at odds with the courts and proper labor market analysis? And why impose an overly strict underutilization standard contrary to that of the courts and accepted statistical practice?

Underutilization requires contractors to invoke good faith corrective efforts including written goals with timetables and policies to be enlisted to achieve them. Federal contractors who believe they have limited allowance to fall short of OFCCP benchmarks may simply hire by quota to avoid any "underutilization." A concomitant cynical observation sometimes offered is that because these employers are contractors, any inefficiencies induced by employment quotas can be passed on to the government—and ultimately taxpayers—with little resistance.

Some observers were particularly concerned about possible quota-inducing effects of the Civil Rights Act of 1990 (which did not become law) and the Civil Rights Act of 1991 that amended Title VII. Ironically, the greatest incentive to self-impose quotas has always fallen on contractors subject to the OFCCP's exceptionally stringent standards. These can be revised or even removed by any administration simply by executive action without congressional vote.

CHAPTER FIVE

Antidiscrimination Policy: Theoretical Considerations

T he prior chapters' examination of recruitment practices and antidiscrimination regulation provides a foundation for public policy proposals. Policy can be based on theoretical arguments, to be discussed in this chapter, or on empirical studies, to be reviewed in chapter 6.

Theoretical considerations of optimal antidiscrimination policy involve general principles common to other analyses of government intervention as well as particular features unique to discrimination. Among the issues to be addressed are efficiency, equity, and administrative costs. These are discussed in turn after sections on basic principles and the dominant employment discrimination paradigm in economics.

5.1 Basic Principles

Economists commonly evaluate public policy options on the basis of two fundamental criteria: efficiency and equity. Efficiency gains occur when more goods and services are produced with the same inputs.[1] Equity increases when income is redistributed from rich to poor. The determination and desirability of equity is far more complex than that of efficiency.[2]

---

1. Only when the increased goods and services are desirable will there unambiguously be an increase in efficiency. If an increase in pollution accompanies an increase in production, then the new outcome might or might not be more efficient than the old, depending on the relative positive valuation of production and negative valuation of pollution.

2. Two major modern treatises in this area are John Rawls, *A Theory of Justice* (Cambridge: Harvard University Press, 1971), esp. chaps. 1–3, proposing to evaluate income distributions by their end-state patterns, focusing on the status of the worst off, and Robert Nozick, *Anarchy, State, and Utopia* (New York: Basic Books, 1974), esp. chap. 7, proposing instead an entitlement theory emphasizing the history of income acquisition and transfer rather than the pattern of the resultant income distribution.

No policy has only efficiency or only equity effects. Policies that focus primarily on efficiency still have some people subsidizing others: Heavy users of tax-financed roads gain from cheaper transport services paid by taxpayers who rarely travel. Similarly, income transfers such as welfare payments, motivated primarily by equity considerations, affect payers' and recipients' incentives to work, and, thereby, the total of goods and services produced. Efficiency-equity trade-offs are common.[3]

A major contribution of economic analysis is the ability to extricate a policy's efficiency and equity effects, including those not foreseen or intended by the policy's proponents. For example, many advocates of minimum wage regulations hope to increase equity by boosting the income of the working poor. However, minimum wage regulations tend to decrease employment opportunities for low-skilled workers and job seekers.[4]

Political philosophy as well as economics affects policy preferences. At one extreme is the libertarian tradition that individuals are free to contract with each other on mutually agreeable terms for whatever reasons provided they eschew force and fraud. Government intervention that proscribes sets of mutually agreeable employer-employee contracts, let alone expands the set of potential employees with whom an employer must negotiate and contract, comprises coercive acts outside the ambit of voluntary association. Libertarians oppugn government-mandated antidiscrimination or affirmative action requirements for private employers:[5] Employers should be free to discriminate or not, to act affirmatively or not, as they prefer.

At the other extreme is a focus on collective rather than individual rights. With a collectivist orientation, the status of groups of citizens, rather than specific transactions between individuals, is paramount. Government can properly intervene on behalf of disadvantaged groups, and antidiscrimination and affirmative action regulation are judged by the extent to which they promote the well-being of their intended beneficiaries.

In general, citizens ranking public policy options will give varying weight to efficiency, equity (including fair treatment of groups within society as well

3. See Arthur M. Okun, *Equality and Efficiency: The Big Tradeoff* (Washington: Brookings Institution, 1975).

4. For reviews of the literature on minimum wage effects, see Charles Brown, Curtis Gilroy, and Andrew Kohen, "The Effect of the Minimum Wage on Employment and Unemployment," *Journal of Economic Literature* 20: 2 (June 1982): 487–528, and Charles Brown, "Minimum Wage Laws: Are They Overrated?" *Journal of Economic Perspectives* 2: 3 (Summer 1988): 133–45. For an identification of winners and losers of minimum wage legislation and an analysis of senators' votes on minimum wage bills showing, in particular, the positive association between yea votes and the extent of unionization across states, see Farrell E. Bloch, "Political Support for Minimum Wage Legislation," *Journal of Labor Research* 1: 2 (Fall 1980): 245–53.

5. For a rigorous exposition of this view, see Epstein, *Forbidden Grounds.*

as the distribution of income and wealth), and the preservation of voluntary individual transactions.

Elected officials generally have more say in the operation of public than of private institutions. Thus, because taxpayers finance their local public libraries, they collectively own them and, through their elected representatives, determine the hours the libraries will be open. In contrast, these representatives less often determine the hours private retail and other establishments are to be open.[6] Indeed, no fundamental libertarian argument can be brought against such intervention in the public sector, because libertarians would not favor the establishment of institutions financed by taxes in the first place, preferring instead to provide services privately.[7] On the other hand, with their focus on outcomes, collectivists would make no major distinction between private and public employers. Given libertarians' opposition to private sector regulation, and collectivists' indifference between rules affecting the public sector and those affecting the private sector, on balance, arguments for employment regulation in general and antidiscrimination or affirmative action coverage in particular are more persuasive when applied to the public than to the private sector. A corollary is that an intermediate level of regulation seems appropriate for private employers who benefit from government protection or subsidy.

Among these employers are public utilities, typically regulated and simultaneously protected from competition; and federal contractors, much of whose business reflects funds of taxpayers, not as individual customers, but rather as collective purchasers whose agents are tax-supported elected officials, their appointees, and civil servants. Additionally, many employers benefit from public programs or expenditures, if not directly, at least indirectly from public provision of the infrastructure; for example, automobile companies are major beneficiaries of government-funded highways that increase the appeal of automobile travel relative to other modes.

Although a vast literature in economics addresses regulatory issues affecting monopolies and other highly concentrated industries, only labor market and not product market concentration is relevant in studying employment: If a utility is the only provider of electric power in a city, the operatives it employs will nonetheless have many alternative job opportunities; thus, although the product market for electric power is maximally concentrated, the labor market for operatives is unconcentrated.

6. Some societies prohibit employers from being open on certain days and before or after certain hours. In the United States, "blue laws" have enjoined retail establishments from being open on Sundays in some states.

7. This statement presumes libertarians oppose all government spending equally. The argument is weakened to the extent libertarians prefer their tax money to be used to provide government services at least cost rather than to satisfy the demographically redistributive predilections of part of the electorate.

Monopsony, a labor market with only one employer, and oligopsony, a labor market with few employers, usually are present only in isolated locations, which job seekers can avoid by moving to densely populated areas. Consequently, monopsony and oligopsony receive far less attention from labor economists than do monopoly and oligopoly from economists specializing in industrial organization. Nonetheless, although monopsonists are few, their insulation from competition will allow them to discriminate more easily than their counterparts in competitive labor markets. Many monopsonists are public employers, such as police and fire departments. Rare examples of private sector monopsonists are small-town southern textile mills.[8]

Opinions on government intervention can be sensitive to many empirical factors, such as the level of poverty and unemployment. If unemployment were more evenly distributed than is shown by the data in tables 3.1, 3.2, and 3.3, and, in particular, were uniformly low, some proponents of antidiscrimination legislation would be less forceful in their support. And if low unemployment rates obviate antidiscrimination policy, then policies that reduce unemployment can be viewed as substitutes for antidiscrimination regulation. Such policies are considered in chapter 7.

Indeed, community organizations, elected officials, and politically active citizens rarely propose labor market intervention on behalf of Asian-Americans, despite prejudice against them, no doubt because Asian-Americans are generally economically successful.[9] How do Asian-Americans, including immigrants with English-language difficulties disqualifying them from many jobs, manage to have an unemployment rate as low as that of whites?[10] One answer is that their relatively high rate of entrepreneurship (see table 3.1) provides word-of-mouth networks that generate jobs for their family members, friends, and neighbors. Another is that Asians' reputation as hard workers stands them in good stead when they compete for jobs.

Yet there is a more basic issue. The overwhelming majority of employers can discriminate against Asians, and Asians can still do well—even without high rates of entrepreneurship. How? By simple arithmetic. If Asian-Americans

8. See p. 143 in James J. Heckman and Brook S. Payner, "Determining the Impact of Federal Antidiscrimination Policy on the Economic Status of Blacks: A Study of South Carolina," *American Economic Review* 79: 1 (March 1989): 138–77, a study further discussed in chapter 6.

9. The overall success of Asian-Americans as a group does not imply the absence of discrimination against each Asian ethnic group in every geographic area. Indeed, the economic status of various Asian-American groups varies considerably. See Harry H. L. Kitano and Roger Daniels, *Asian Americans: Emerging Minorities* (Englewood Cliffs, N.J.: Prentice-Hall, 1988).

10. Table 3.1 shows that, in 1980, Asian-Americans' unemployment rate was 4.73 percent (males, 4.29 percent; females, 5.22 percent), while whites' was 5.78 percent (males, 5.86 percent; females, 5.69 percent). Unpublished Census data indicate that in 1990, Asian-Americans' unemployment rate was 5.31 percent (males, 5.12 percent; females, 5.53 percent), while whites' was 5.21 percent (males, 5.34 percent; females, 5.04 percent).

constitute 5 percent of the labor market, they need only find the 5 percent of jobs for which they will be considered. Thus, if 95 percent of job vacancies are off-limits for Asian-Americans, Asian-Americans can still be fully employed by focusing their efforts on the remaining employers.

If antidiscrimination laws need not apply universally to ensure jobs for all, to whom should they apply? The arguments presented previously suggest that public employers might be at the top of the list, followed by federal contractors. Are there any other subsets of employers to whom the law should or should not particularly apply?

Small employers are already a group exempt from Title VII of the Civil Rights Act: The act defines covered employers as those with at least fifteen employees, reduced from twenty-five with passage of the Equal Employment Opportunity Act of 1972.[11] The OFCCP's mandate applies to federal contractor employers of fifty or more. Although no strong argument can be advanced for a specific number below which the law should not apply, observers recognize that regulations on small firms are especially onerous,[12] and that businesses started by family members or close friends will naturally often be racially or ethnically homogeneous with the initial employees found within the owners' personal networks.

Won't applying antidiscrimination laws only to some sectors of the labor market, such as public but not private employers, bring about segregation of the work force? Perhaps. However, firms not covered by these laws would thereby not be *prohibited* from hiring members of certain ethnic groups: Having no antidiscrimination and affirmative action regulation is a far cry from enforcing segregation. Moreover, firms serving ethnically diverse customers have clear incentives to hire correspondingly diverse work forces if salespeople and others are more effective doing business with those culturally similar to them.

So far no distinction has been made between policies proscribing discrimination and those requiring affirmative action. The former undoubtedly have greater support than the latter. It is not easy to imagine a proponent of affirmative action who would oppose laws forbidding discrimination; on the other hand, many who favor antidiscrimination laws in the hope of achieving a level playing field for all are opposed to affirmative action on grounds that it favors some groups over others.

Similarly, employers' disparate treatment practices are undoubtedly more

11. Some legislators involved in drafting these 1972 amendments wanted to cover employers with as few as eight employees. See *Legislative History of the Equal Employment Opportunity Act of 1972*, p. 444.

12. Ibid., p. 1857. In general, small employers are less heavily regulated than large ones, both by size exemptions and regulatory agencies' enforcement practices. See Brown, Hamilton, and Medoff, *Employers Large and Small*, chap. 9.

widely objectionable than their policies with disparate impact. Again, it is difficult to conceive of a supporter of laws prohibiting disparate impact who would prefer that the legal system ignore the more blatant acts of disparate treatment; on the other hand, some who are offended by disparate treatment nevertheless wish to allow employers to determine their own policies and practices, and are thus not sympathetic to specific or general interventionist arguments based on disparate impact.

In summary, a stronger case exists for antidiscrimination coverage of public than of private employers, with an intermediate argument for federal contractors and employers in regulated industries; for groups with high unemployment rates than for groups economically well off; for larger than smaller employers; for basic antidiscrimination law than affirmative action requirements; and for prohibitions against disparate treatment than those against disparate impact. Of course, some may favor regulation of all or none of these. Others may wish to consider the efficiency and equity arguments of sections 5.3 and 5.4.

5.2 The Discrimination Paradigm

The theoretical and empirical studies in the economics of discrimination literature have focused primarily on pay. The arguments at the beginning of chapter 3 concerning the varying implications of employer, employee, and consumer discrimination for racial segregation and hiring, and the section 3.1 analyses of statistical discrimination, are adapted from models where the fundamental employer decision is not whom to hire, but what rates of pay to offer members of different groups.[13]

The empirical literature also has focused heavily on pay and earnings differentials by race and sex.[14] Researchers seek to explain these differences by such factors as education and work history. In most studies a difference by race and sex remains no matter how many explanatory factors are adduced.[15] And no consensus exists on the extent to which these unexplained wage differentials reflect discrimination, as opposed to elusive dimensions of labor quality.

Recruitment and hiring discrimination will be directly reflected not in pay differences but in variations in group unemployment rates such as those presented in tables 3.1–3.3. The occasional study of unemployment rates by race

13. As noted in chapter 3, the seminal treatise is Gary Becker's *The Economics of Discrimination.*

14. For a summary of these studies see Glen G. Cain, "The Economic Analysis of Labor Market Discrimination: A Survey," chap. 13, pp. 693–785, in Orley Ashenfelter and Richard Layard, eds., *Handbook of Labor Economics,* vol. 2 (Amsterdam: North-Holland, 1986).

15. Exceptions include parity for young black and white male college graduates in the early seventies, but not thereafter. See Smith and Welch, "Black Economic Progress after Myrdal," table 28, p. 556.

and sex demonstrates that only some of these differences can be explained by such factors as education and labor market experience.[16]

In any event, the standard paradigm predicts that discrimination eventually will vanish. Because the lack of demand from discriminating employers depresses the pay of blacks below that of comparable whites, nondiscriminating competitors will hire blacks, thereby gaining advantages in the form of extra profits from employing productive black labor at depressed wages. Over time, as the discriminating employers are not able to compete with their more profitable nondiscriminating competitors, they will go out of business (or become nondiscriminators) and blacks' pay will rise eventually to parity with that of whites.[17]

The conclusion among many researchers that pay—and unemployment rate—differentials by race and sex continue to reflect at least some discrimination strongly suggests that discrimination is not vanishing. Among the explanations for the persistence of these differentials after factors such as education and experience have been held constant are: (1) no or too few nondiscriminating employers are present to drive the discriminators out of business; (2) the apparent pay and employment differentials reflect not discrimination but differences in labor quality that were not explicitly taken into account in the studies; and (3) the competitive model underlying the conclusion that discrimination will vanish does not depict the economy very well. More complex explanations are based on the lack of perfect information about potential employees,[18] to which condition the statistical discrimination models discussed in section 3.1 are a response, and the fixed costs of hiring individuals (which should inhibit the speed of discrimination's decline, but not prevent its eventual disappearance).

To my knowledge, no one has investigated the relationship between these fixed costs of hiring (and firing), rates of employee turnover, and entry and exit rates of firms from industries. Within the standard competitive model, it may be that firms so frequently experience shifting demand and supply conditions for labor (including those induced by changes in the demand for and supply of the goods and services they produce) that discriminating and nondiscriminating firms are rarely directly competitive long enough for employment discrim-

16. See, for example, Farrell E. Bloch and Sharon P. Smith, "Human Capital and Labor Market Employment," *Journal of Human Resources* 12: 4 (Fall 1977): 550–60.

17. This process obviously cannot work in a monopsonistic market and will work more slowly in an oligopsonistic one. See also the brief discussion in the previous section.

18. These more complex phenomena are discussed by Kenneth J. Arrow, "Models of Job Discrimination," chap. 2 in Anthony H. Pascal, ed., *Racial Discrimination in Economic Life* (Lexington, Mass.: Lexington Books, D. C. Heath, 1972), and "The Theory of Discrimination," pp. 3–33 in Orley Ashenfelter and Albert Rees, eds., *Discrimination in Labor Markets* (Princeton, N.J.: Princeton University Press, 1973). A more technical argument presented in these articles, based on the economic concept of nonconvexities, implies segregation of workers and does not directly address the disappearance of discrimination.

ination to vanish. Thus, rather than a discriminating and a nondiscriminating employer selling the same product under stable supply and demand conditions, each may be affected by such factors as production and sale of other products, personnel issues, financial management, and difficulties with suppliers or customers, all of which can overwhelm their different propensities to hire minorities. Moreover, with job and ownership changes, discriminating and nondiscriminating decision-makers may replace each other, thus reversing discrimination eradication processes already in motion.[19] Thus, discriminating and nondiscriminating firms are not fighting a duel, but rather a series of battles in which the economic actors, ground rules, and conditions are in states of flux.

It is of course possible to reconcile the persistence of the table 3.1., 3.2, and 3.3 unemployment rate differences with the basic paradigm by concluding that only a very slow decline in employment discrimination, rather than its rapid elimination, can occur. Moreover, the statistical discrimination arguments based on imperfect information (section 3.1), and the preference for word-of-mouth recruitment (sections 2.1 and 2.5), in conjunction with societal segregation and low rates of minority entrepreneurship (section 3.2), explain persistent poor labor market outcomes for minorities even when employers bear no animus toward them.

At any rate, the apparent persistence of discrimination has led many economists and others to be sympathetic to government intervention in the labor market on behalf of protected classes. Mindful of the possibility that anti-discrimination regulation itself may have effects other than those which its proponents hope for or intend, economists have not simply assumed that government intervention will solve the problem of discrimination while inducing no other distortions. Chapter 6 focuses on the labor market effects of antidiscrimination and affirmative action programs in the United States, giving particular attention to the lack of contraction in black-white unemployment rates during the almost thirty years since passage of the Civil Rights Act of 1964.

5.3 Efficiency

The primary efficiency argument supporting policies seeking to counter recruitment discrimination is that government intervention will motivate employers to consider applicants, otherwise ignored, who will match well with

---

19. An analogy may be helpful. Assume a model predicts that open bottles left outdoors on rainy days eventually will be completely filled with rainwater. Further suppose that water-filled bottles are never observed. It may still be the case that the process of rain filling bottles is occurring, but that other factors—such as bottles being broken, emptied, or taken indoors sufficiently frequently—prevent its completion. This process is modeled, not by firms competing under static conditions, but rather by firms moving in the direction of continually changing equilibria. See Israel Kirzner, *Competition and Entrepreneurship* (Chicago: University of Chicago Press, 1973).

employers' job vacancies. Nonetheless, it is impossible to construct an example where a government-induced match of an employee and a job opportunity will be *Pareto-superior,* that is, increasing the welfare of at least one party, while not decreasing the welfare of anyone else.

Assume the government prohibits word-of-mouth or targeted recruitment and requires a company to publicize a vacancy to black as well as white job seekers. Or, alternatively, assume the government requires affirmative action in the form of targeted recruitment directed at black job seekers. The eventual result is that the employer hires a black instead of a white.

The unemployment of the white job seeker who would have been hired under the preregulation recruitment policy prevents this series of events from being Pareto-superior. The scenario can be Pareto-superior only if the white is somehow compensated, perhaps by being hired into a job that is preferred to the job taken by the black (and we would have to make some strong assumptions about the lack of earnings losses incurred by the individual who would have been hired into the job taken by the white and those subsequently displaced by this chain of hires). The simple substitution of a black worker for a white worker cannot be justified on grounds of Pareto-superiority, although perhaps on the basis of some externality and equity arguments to be discussed below.

Furthermore, for the employer to be better off with the black hire, it is necessary but not sufficient that the black worker be more productive than the white would have been. The black's productivity advantage must more than compensate the extra recruitment and evaluation costs incurred by the employer. Whatever the productivity of the black hire, a proponent of unregulated markets would argue that the employer clearly is worse off being regulated by being forced into an option not freely chosen. That is, if nondiscriminating employers knew of exceptionally productive blacks worth extra recruitment and evaluation efforts, they would have sought them out without government intervention. That the employers did not reflects reasoned cost-benefit calculations, admittedly based on imperfect information, that the government should not counteract. To put it differently, some would reject in principle the idea that government regulators will induce employers to make efficiency-enhancing decisions that would not previously have occurred to them.

Suppose the employer prefers to discriminate, and government regulation has forced the hire of a black that otherwise would not occur. Is the overall policy then a better idea? On efficiency grounds, it is even worse than if the employer were not a discriminator, because all factors remain the same as before except that a discriminating white employer also objects to the presence of a black employee on grounds of racial prejudice or preference.

It is exceedingly difficult to find government policies that are Pareto-superior because intervention induces choices other than those made voluntarily—and voluntary associations are arranged because all parties expect to benefit, although individuals are sometimes worse off after a transaction that they expected would improve their situation. So long as only one person is worse off, a policy is not Pareto-superior. Not surprisingly, economists inimical to government intervention stress Pareto-superiority and the impossibility of comparing one person's gains against another's losses to determine a net societal gain or loss. In practice, many individuals are willing to argue for or against certain policies by weighing the policies' effects on the various gainers and losers, and will support policies they believe are nearly Pareto-superior in the sense that the losers, perhaps after some compensation, suffer only small losses.

Indeed, similar arguments cannot establish Pareto-superiority even for the policy of outlawing racial segregation requirements in the workplace. Although black job seekers and white employers would be better off with the expanded choices possible after repealing segregation, some white workers would be worse off by no longer having job opportunities restricted to them. The welfare loss of white workers competing directly with blacks prevents segregation's repeal from being a Pareto-superior policy.

In principle, black job seekers could overcome statistical discrimination (see section 3.1) by presenting evidence that their productivity was higher than that of others similarly situated with respect to education and experience. Interestingly, however, the theory of disparate impact, by devaluing the use of information about job seekers, precludes capable black applicants from presenting certain impressive credentials or the ability to score well on tests as a way to surmount the statistical discrimination against blacks as a group. Because employers' general use of these criteria in hiring decisions might increase their exposure to class action disparate impact lawsuits, they must be wary of considering such information on behalf of a specific applicant. In contrast, one of the common arguments for government intervention is to provide—certainly not to suppress—information. For example, packaged foods sold in the United States are required by law to list their ingredients because of the presumed difficulty consumers would have in acquiring such knowledge on their own.[20]

Policies often have *externalities,* indirect effects on others besides the direct participants. For example, when black job seekers are hired, their black friends, relatives, and neighbors benefit from accessibility to new word-of-mouth job-seeking networks. Furthermore, each such hire counters the perception among blacks that the level of discrimination against them renders futile

20. A counter to this argument is that if consumers demanded detailed labeling, profit-seeking food companies would provide it as an advantage over competitors. If consumers did not demand labeling, the legal requirements to label would reflect increased costs, which would be passed on to consumers as higher prices. And if only some consumers wanted this information, they could subscribe to organizations analyzing the composition of foods.

Table 5.1   Employees in Contractor and EEO-1 Reporting Firms

	Number	Percentage of BLS figure	Percentage of Census figure
Employees of			
Federal contractors	27,435,781	30.6	23.7
Establishments filing EEO-1 reports	42,116,528	47.0	36.4
Bureau of Labor Statistics count	89,702,612	100.0	77.5
Total civilian employment	115,681,202	129.0	100.0

Sources: Employees in establishments of federal contractors and firms filing EEO-1 reports, submitted in the first quarter of 1990, unpublished data provided by U.S. Department of Labor, Office of Federal Contract Compliance Programs. Bureau of Labor Statistics data for March 1989 from U.S. Equal Employment Opportunity Commission, *Job Patterns for Minorities and Women in Private Industry*, 1989, which excludes employees of government, and of private and public educational institutions, and residents of Hawaii (to be comparable with EEOC contractor and EEO-1 data in the same publication), multiplied by 1.0046 to include employees in Hawaii, and by 1.016, the increase in employees on EEO-1 reports between 1989 and 1990, to be comparable with 1990 data in table. Total civilian employment from unpublished 1990 Census data provided by U.S. Department of Commerce, Bureau of the Census.

both present job search and skill acquisition in preparation for future employment. Blacks' incentives to acquire job-related skills may therefore increase, and black high school and college attendance and graduation rates may rise in response. White employer-black employee combinations may also contribute to general interracial amity. In addition, assuming the matches are good ones, newly enlightened employers may cast their recruitment nets wider to include the black community when future vacancies occur. They will also be able to exploit their black hires' word-of-mouth networks, and thereby have low-cost access to a relatively untapped source of potential productive employees.

Unfortunate externalities of affirmative action policies include disincentives for its beneficiaries to acquire skills, and devaluation of protected-class members' achievements. Minorities believing that their labor market rewards will accrue primarily to their ethnicity will have reduced incentives to acquire job skills—similarly to minority workers expecting employer discriminatory decisions to override skill assessment. Furthermore, an employer reviewing a minority applicant's work history may attribute various positions and accomplishments to affirmative action rather than to the competence of the applicant. Thus, some applicants may be rejected for jobs that they might have been offered if affirmative action policies were not perceived to have been in force under previous employers.[21] Ironically, most employers have no affirmative action plans. Although some organizations voluntarily adopt them, the bulk of employers with affirmative action plans are federal contractors. And, as table 5.1 shows, federal contractors' employees comprise less than one-quarter of the work force.

21. For an examination of these and other phenomena, particularly in the context of education, see Stephen Carter, *Reflections of an Affirmative Action Baby* (New York: Basic Books, 1991).

5.4 Equity

Four basic equity arguments provide support for antidiscrimination and affirmative action regulation. Three of these emphasize equality of results, i.e., redistribution of income, and one focuses on equality of opportunity, i.e., equal
access to earning possibilities. Because they are based on comparisons between groups, and downplay or ignore individual variation within and across
groups, the arguments will appeal most strongly to those with a collectivist
perspective.

First, antidiscrimination and affirmative action regulation has been justified on grounds of past discrimination, especially the humiliation African-
Americans endured as slaves and later as second-class citizens subject to
segregation and voting barriers. From a collectivist point of view, blacks and
other minorities deserve recompense, and any policies that redistribute wealth
or income-earning opportunities to them from whites will begin to redress past
wrongs. The corresponding libertarian solution, that the descendants of slave
owners and other beneficiaries of crimes against African-Americans should
compensate their victims directly, outside the labor market, is much more
problematic to implement: In particular, the high cost of discovering and assessing past crimes provides one justification for statutes of limitation. In any
case, recent white and black immigrants, among others, would be outside the
loop of these compensatory property or income exchanges.

Second, proponents of income redistribution may prefer antidiscrimination
and affirmative action regulation on the grounds that it serves that goal, albeit
inefficiently and indirectly.[22] Indeed, if income redistribution is the goal, why
limit it to those in the labor force who can allege discrimination or take advantage of affirmative action, and ignore other labor force participants, not to
mention the retired, those seriously disabled, and children? Moreover, affirmative action sometimes will transfer income to minorities wealthier than the
whites over whom they are chosen.

A third argument for these programs highlights the gains in social utility accompanying the reduction of gaps between racial and ethnic groups' economic
status. In particular, racial and ethnic amity may improve if blacks, Hispanics,
and American Indians are no longer disproportionately represented below the
poverty line.

Finally, some favor antidiscrimination but not affirmative action regulation
because they wish to ensure equality of opportunity, but not to guarantee
equality of results. A basic sense of fairness motivates a desire for a level playing field on which all Americans can compete. Nonetheless, some affirmative
action may be needed even to achieve a level playing field. For example,

22. Analogously, many trade unions advocate government-provided fringe benefits such as Social Security and health insurance that increase the overall compensation of workers and thus
indirectly serve the union policy goal of redistributing employer profits to workers.

because blacks are geographically clustered, their personal networks consist largely of black persons, many of whom attended segregated schools or otherwise experienced discrimination. Also, relatively few blacks are entrepreneurs (see section 3.2). Thus, blacks' word-of-mouth networks are not generally as fruitful in generating jobs as are comparable networks for whites. Affirmative action recruitment is thus necessary to provide equal opportunity for black job seekers.[23]

5.5 Administrative Costs

One of the implications of antidiscrimination and affirmative action regulation is that employers may modify their employment practices and policies and make employment decisions different from—and less efficient and less profitable than—those they would otherwise choose. Additionally, depending on the nature of the regulatory apparatus in force, employers may have to incur costs of filing reports; maintaining records; and retaining equal employment opportunity specialists, consultants, and counsel both to monitor adherence to regulations and to resolve employee complaints ranging from minor grievances to lawsuits.[24] Private employers in the United States with at least one hundred employees have to submit annual EEO-1 reports to the EEOC, and federal contractors must in addition produce and execute affirmative action plans. All covered employers are required to maintain applications of rejected applicants as well as those of applicants to whom they offered jobs for at least a year after the date of the hiring decision.[25] Employers losing or settling lawsuits often are obliged to hire or to employ specific percentages of protected-class members or to pay damages to plaintiffs.

The regulatory agencies themselves generate direct and indirect costs, including those of drafting, discussing, and lobbying for amendments to the law. Moreover, specialist employees and consultants of regulatory agencies and interest groups, like those working for regulated employers, have opportunity costs: If they were not training and working on discrimination issues, they would be able to produce other goods and services. A similar example obtains for the Internal Revenue Service: If the income tax system were simplified or replaced by sales or value-added taxes, the need for IRS personnel as well as

23. This basic argument is made, but stressing education and parental transfer of productive characteristics rather than networks for job seeking, by Glenn C. Loury, "Is Equal Opportunity Enough?" *American Economic Review* 71: 2 (May 1981): 122–26, and "Why Should We Care about Group Inequality?" chap. 9, pp. 268–90, in Steven Shulman and William Darity, Jr., eds., *Racial Inequality in the U.S. Labor Market* (Middletown, Conn.: Wesleyan University Press, 1989).

24. The OFCCP's impact on employer costs is noted at the end of section 6.2. That of the EEOC has not been similarly studied, to my knowledge.

25. 29 Code of Federal Regulations 1602. Before August 26, 1991, the applicant retention period was only six months.

for private accountants would drop precipitously, freeing these individuals to produce other goods and services.

As a rule, those employed as a result of a regulatory structure have a strong self-interest in maintaining and promoting that structure. These very individuals are the ones best acquainted with the details of the systems in which they work and are often the constituents of expert task forces. Accordingly, it is unlikely that labor lawyers, consultants who prepare affirmative action plans, and human resources professionals specializing in equal employment opportunity issues will recommend that the antidiscrimination and affirmative action regulations be curtailed or abolished, just as most accountants would not support abolition of the income tax in favor of other taxes or simplification of the tax forms to an extent that their services generally would not be needed.

Whatever the appeal of the efficiency and equity arguments presented above, they must be balanced against an appreciation of private and public direct and indirect administrative and compliance costs. Without considering costs, the idea of completely eradicating discrimination is appealing. Yet because of the attendant costs, few people recommend total eradication of societal ills.

For example, thousands of individuals die annually from highway accidents. Yet rather than proscribing automobile travel, policymakers seek only to increase safety by encouraging such policies as requiring the use of seat belts and imposing strong penalties against those driving under the influence of alcohol or drugs. Indeed, few people recommend even such policies as regularly scheduled driving tests or increases in the highway police force: The infringement on liberty and the added costs to pay for these services exceed most citizens' valuation of the expected benefits.

Similarly, those favoring regulation of employment generally stop short of wanting to monitor every employer decision and paying the costs of an expanded regulatory bureaucracy to do so. The intrusion on the freedom of the business community and the concomitant reductions in efficiency are critical considerations. Proponents of regulation are generally comfortable with an intermediate approach. One's opinion on whether and how much to regulate may depend not only on the theoretical issues discussed in this chapter, but on the actual effects of the policies in force—to be considered in chapter 6.

CHAPTER SIX

The Effects of
Antidiscrimination Programs

Policy proposals may be based on the actual impact of antidiscrimination and affirmative action regulation rather than on the theoretical considerations noted in the previous chapter. Accordingly, this chapter reviews empirical evidence on these programs, and discusses policy proposals based on that evidence. In addition to the usual focus on public policy, a section is devoted to private policy, the set of actions available to individual job seekers, employers, and concerned citizens.

Economists have studied the effects on employment and pay of Title VII of the Civil Rights Act and the Department of Labor's affirmative action–oriented federal contract compliance program. Because Title VII applies only to employers of fifteen or more (twenty-five or more prior to March 24, 1973, the effective date of the Equal Employment Opportunity Act of 1972), one could in principle study the employment rates for various groups in covered and noncovered (i.e., large and small) firms. Evidence that the level of Title VII enforcement was correlated with greater increases of employment rates of protected-class members in large than in small firms would support the hypothesis that Title VII is effective. Focusing on all covered employers rather than those who have been sued recognizes the larger group of employers who have incentives to comport with Title VII regulations to avoid litigation. However, because small noncovered firms are primarily family businesses recruiting largely through personal referrals, they cannot provide a sizable comparison group with the potential to employ many minorities to which Title VII does not apply. Thus, study of the impact of Title VII must involve time-series analysis, tracking changes across years, rather than cross-section studies of employers at a point in time.

On the other hand, analyses of the effect of the OFCCP's regulations for federal contractors are conceptually easier to address, because researchers can study a large set of federal contractors and noncontractors. Interpreting contractor-noncontractor differences raises the possibility that contractors' nondiscrimination and affirmative action obligations simply engender shifts of employees from one sector to another: Protected-class members who, absent the OFCCP, would have worked for noncontractors more easily found jobs with contractors, with the reverse obtaining for white males. The economy-wide net result may have been minimal.

Studies of the impact of Title VII and the federal contract compliance programs are summarized in sections 6.1 and 6.2. Section 6.3 attempts to reconcile these studies with tables 3.1, 3.2, and 3.3, which depict a constant or slightly widening gap in black-white unemployment differentials over time. Sections 6.4 and 6.5 address private and public policy.

6.1 Effects of Title VII of the Civil Rights Act of 1964

The Civil Rights Act of 1964 had three concomitant effects: (1) repeal of the southern "Jim Crow" laws [1] enforcing segregation in such institutions as transportation, schools, parks, theaters, and restaurants; (2) promulgation of a federal policy of nondiscrimination; and (3) lawsuits and enforcement actions against employers. Thus, its differential impact on blacks in the South in the late 1960s and early 1970s relative to that in other regions or during later years provides a measure of the first two of these effects—the elimination of Jim Crow and the federal government's nondiscrimination mandate—on the behavior of southern whites, who, for the first time, were living in a society in which discrimination was clearly outlawed.

Because Jim Crow did not generally address the labor market, its effects there were indirect. If blacks and whites were customarily required to use separate restrooms and water fountains, then an employer wishing to mirror society's patterns would have to install more facilities with an integrated than with a segregated work force. Because a segregated workplace is cheaper to accommodate in the sense of requiring half the personal facilities of a comparable integrated establishment, some employers would hire only whites. Employers seeking to integrate before 1964 might also incur the retaliation of local public officials in the form of stricter inspections and refusals of permits.[2] With passage of the Civil Rights Act of 1964, separate facilities became illegal and workplace integration more feasible. Moreover, the laws themselves elevated equality to a social desideratum and placed a federal imprimatur on the policy of hiring blacks into positions previously closed to them. The federal government's mandate of nondiscrimination alone may have altered behavior, and may have been responsible for considerable impact of Title VII independent of

1. For a history of the origins and development of Jim Crow, see C. Vann Woodward, *The Strange Career of Jim Crow,* 3d rev. ed. (Oxford: Oxford University Press, 1974).
2. Epstein, *Forbidden Grounds,* p. 246.

its enforcement. Indeed, "[s]ubstantial numbers of Southern employers appear to have been willing to gain access to the cheap supply of black labor, but required the excuse of the federal pressure to defy long-standing community norms regarding employment of blacks."[3] It is also possible that the laws reflected, as well as induced, changing attitudes, in particular, greater emphasis on economic growth.[4] Additionally, ratification of Article XXIV to the Constitution[5] proscribing poll taxes and passage of the Voting Rights Act of 1965[6] increased the likelihood that blacks' preferences would affect local policy; presumably, the greater blacks' political representation, the more likely the eventual demise of Jim Crow, even without the Civil Rights Act of 1964.

Most of the gain in blacks' relative (i.e., compared with whites') economic status since passage of Title VII occurred in the late 1960s and early 1970s and was heavily concentrated in the South: Between 1966 and 1970, employers' ratio of black male to white male employees increased in the South by 20 percent more than in the rest of the country.[7] And the probability that a firm with no black workers in 1966 employed at least one black worker in 1970 was 14 percent greater in the South than in any other region.[8]

Similarly, an analysis of males' 1963–87 hourly earnings revealed: "For the non-South, there is virtually no improvement in the earnings deficit of black

3. Quote from p. 1605 of John J. Donohue III and James Heckman, "Continuous versus Episodic Change: The Impact of Civil Rights Policy on the Economic Status of Blacks," *Journal of Economic Literature* 29: 4 (December 1991): 1603–43.

4. In the introduction to Elizabeth Jacoway and David R. Colburn, eds., *Southern Businessmen and Desegregation* (Baton Rouge: Louisiana State University Press, 1982), Elizabeth Jacoway writes (p. 3), "Nonetheless, although these articles contain a variety of interpretations of the nature and meaning of the business elite's response to desegregation, taken together these articles do suggest that the South's white businessmen yielded to the demands for change because of a fundamental reordering of their priorities: although the maintenance of white supremacy remained a cherished objective, somewhere along the way it slipped from its traditionally dominant position and the primary objective for the South's business leaders became economic growth."

5. Article XXIV, passed by Congress on August 27, 1962, and ratified by the states on January 23, 1964, protected citizens' right to vote from federal or state abridgment on grounds of failure to pay poll taxes or any other tax.

6. Public Law 89-110, effective August 6, 1965. The law outlawed restrictive practices such as literacy tests, whose implementation by local southern officials had suppressed black voter registration; provided for federal examiners and election observers; and made illegal any changes in the law that would adversely affect minority voters. As a result, the proportion of blacks eligible to vote increased sharply in the mid-1960s. See Steven F. Lawson, *Black Ballots: Voting Rights in the South* (New York: Columbia University Press, 1976).

7. Orley Ashenfelter and James Heckman, "The Effect of an Anti-Discrimination Program," pp. 46–84 in Orley Ashenfelter and James Blum, eds., *Evaluating the Labor-Market Effects of Social Programs* (Princeton, N.J.: Industrial Relations Section, Princeton University, 1976), table 4, p. 66.

8. Ibid., table 7, pp. 74–75.

men over the twenty-four year period. In contrast, Southern blacks experienced sharp relative wage gains over the decade 1965–1975, with virtual stagnation thereafter."[9] Other studies have supported the conclusion that blacks' gains were largest in the South.[10] And an investigation of earnings and employment in the 1980s concluded that "the era of relative black economic advance ended in the mid-1970s."[11]

Most interestingly, blacks' rapid progress occurred only during the decade following the passage of Title VII when antidiscrimination cases in general and hiring cases in particular were not common. Indeed, although plaintiffs in the 1960s sued firms on grounds of gross exclusion of blacks, hiring lawsuits were limited because the theory of disparate impact was not articulated until *Griggs* in 1971, the EEOC had no power to sue until 1972, and applicants were not protected by Title VII until 1972 (see section 4.1).

The EEOC's budget and staffing reflect its expanding power (table 6.1). Between (fiscal years) 1966 and 1976, the commission's budget authorization increased twentyfold in current dollars and tenfold in constant dollars. By the end of the 1970s, the budget had doubled again in current dollars and was about a third higher in constant dollars. Throughout the 1980s, budgets rose slowly in current dollars to maintain a stable constant dollar level. Authorized staffing was 314 in 1966 and 1967, about 1,000 in 1971, and about 2,000 in 1973, and rose to its peak of 3,752 in 1979, declining to about 3,000 thereafter.

Consistent with this pattern and the extent of the law, the number of EEOC hiring charges each fiscal year increased dramatically after passage of the 1972 amendment, reaching a plateau by the mid-1970s.[12] Annual hiring complaints filed by all plaintiffs also appear to have risen sharply in the early 1970s, peaking in the mid-1970s and declining slightly thereafter.[13] The total number of employment discrimination cases per year increased sharply after 1970, then leveled off in the mid-1980s.[14] Annual class action requests in employment discrimination litigation surged through most of the 1970s, then declined precipitously near the end of the decade, returning to their 1970 level by the early 1980s.[15]

9. Donohue and Heckman, "Continuous versus Episodic Change," p. 1610.

10. See, for example, Richard B. Freeman, "Changes in the Labor Market for Black Americans, 1948–72," and "Comments and Discussion," *Brookings Papers on Economic Activity,* 1973, no. 1, pp. 67–131, esp. p. 124 and p. 128, and "Black Economic Progress after 1964: Who Has Gained and Why?" chap. 8, pp. 247–94, in Sherwin Rosen, ed., *Studies in Labor Markets* (Chicago: University of Chicago Press, 1981), esp. fig. 8.1, pp. 278–79.

11. Bound and Freeman, "What Went Wrong?" p. 202.

12. See fig. 6, p. 1016, in John J. Donohue III and Peter Siegelman, "The Changing Nature of Employment Discrimination Litigation," *Stanford Law Review* 43: 5 (May 1991): 983–1033.

13. Ibid., fig. 7, p. 1016.

14. Ibid., figs. 1 and 2, p. 986.

15. Ibid., pp. 1019–21.

Table 6.1   Budget and Staffing of the
Equal Employment Opportunity Commission

| Fiscal year | Appropriation | | Staff |
	Current $ (000)	Constant $ (000)	
1966	3,250	10,031	314
1967	5,240	15,689	314
1968	6,655	19,124	389
1969	9,120	24,850	579
1970	13,400	34,536	780
1971	16,185	39,963	910
1972	23,000	55,024	1,325
1973	32,000	72,072	1,909
1974	44,400	90,061	2,388
1975	56,146	104,361	2,384
1976	63,659	111,879	2,584
1977	70,513	116,358	2,487
1978	84,550	129,678	2,837
1979	106,750	147,039	3,752
1980	124,562	151,168	3,390
1981	144,610	159,087	3,358
1982	144,739	149,989	3,166
1983	147,421	148,013	3,084
1984	154,039	148,257	3,044
1985	163,655	152,096	3,097
1986	165,000	150,547	3,017
1987	169,529	149,233	2,941
1988	179,812	151,997	3,168
1989	180,712	145,735	2,970
1990	184,926	141,489	2,853
1991	201,930	148,260	2,796
1992	211,271	150,693	2,791

Sources: *Equal Employment Opportunity Commission Annual Reports, 1966–1989* and unpublished data (including revisions of data in annual reports) for current dollar fiscal year authorized budget and authorized full-time equivalent staffing; *Economic Report of the President, 1993*, table B-58, for consumer price index allowing transformation of current dollar budgets into constant (1982–84) dollar budgets. Supplementary budget allocation for fifth quarter of fiscal year 1976 not included.

Early studies of the impact of Title VII correlated measures of EEOC enforcement, such as the number of charges filed with the commission or the agency's dollar expenditures, with improvements in minority status.[16] However, the level of EEOC enforcement at different times or across areas may

16. For a more detailed analysis of early studies, see pp. 252–57 and 259–62 in Richard Butler and James J. Heckman, "The Government's Impact on the Labor Market Status of Black Americans: A Critical Review," chap. 9, pp. 235–81, in Leonard J. Hausman et al., eds., *Equal Rights and Industrial Relations* (Madison: Industrial Relations Research Association, 1977).

be a response to the perceived level of discrimination rather than a cause of it. Thus, the combination of high EEOC enforcement and low minority employment or pay may reflect the EEOC's intervention in response to possibly illegal employment practices rather than the inadequacy of its efforts. Alternatively, if applicants' or employees' appreciation of their rights under Title VII obtains only at firms with a threshold representation of protected-class members, a positive correlation across employers between the incidence of litigation and minority representation would not reflect only the impact of Title VII. And, analogously to nonunion employers increasing pay in response to the threat of unionization, firms may hire minorities in an attempt to preclude future EEOC intervention.

Furthermore, over time, blacks' employment and earnings prospects were enhanced by their increasing quantity and quality of education.[17] Also, the expansion of income transfer programs disproportionately removed low-skilled blacks from the labor market, increasing the average earnings of those who remained.[18] And efforts to counter pay disparities induced a fundamental antinomy into antidiscrimination policy: Enforcement of higher minority pay discourages (the consequently more expensive) minority employment.

The 1966 to 1978 increase in the representation of blacks, especially black women, among employees of manufacturing firms filing EEO-1 reports each year was positively correlated with the number of Title VII class action lawsuits per corporation in the same industry and state.[19] The impact was most striking in professional and managerial positions. Interpretation of these results is complicated by the considerations noted above and the possibility that the increased black employment may have reflected a corresponding decrease in the 26 percent of manufacturing firms of a size below EEO-1 reporting levels—or in other industries.

Might the post-1964 improvement of blacks' economic status in the United States be the result of factors other than antidiscrimination regulation? Approximately 15 to 20 percent of relative black income gains is attributable to schooling quality improvements, in particular, the retirement from the labor force of blacks educated in segregated schools and their replacement by younger blacks whose educational experiences were closer to those of whites. Another 20 to 25 percent can be explained by the narrowing racial gap in years

17. David Card and Alan B. Krueger, "School Quality and Black-White Relative Earnings: A Direct Assessment," *Quarterly Journal of Economics* 107: 1 (February 1992): 151–200, conclude that improvements in the relative quality of black schools explain 20 percent of the narrowing of the black-white earnings gap between 1960 and 1980.

18. James J. Heckman, "The Impact of Government on the Economic Status of Black Americans," chap. 3, pp. 50–80, in Shulman and Darity, eds., *Racial Inequality in the Labor Market*.

19. Jonathan S. Leonard, "Antidiscrimination or Reverse Discrimination: The Impact of Changing Demographics, Title VII, and Affirmative Action on Productivity," *Journal of Human Resources* 19: 2 (Spring 1984): 145–74.

of education. Finally, 10 to 20 percent of the earnings difference reduction is the result of the withdrawal from the labor force of blacks with low earnings capacity. Black interregional migration, an important factor earlier in this century, played no significant role after 1965.[20]

Thus, 45 to 65 percent of blacks' relative income progress can be explained by conventional factors, and 35 to 55 percent is presumably due to federal pressure, including Title VII and the federal contract compliance program. Because these programs were not in full gear during the period of blacks' greatest advances in the South in the late 1960s and early 1970s, the picture is consistent with southern white employers' discontinuous change in behavior accompanying the demise of Jim Crow and a federal policy of nondiscrimination—independent of lawsuits and other enforcement efforts. Later, when lawsuits were more numerous and enforcement efforts stronger, blacks' economic status did not improve.

Nevertheless, the impact of specific antidiscrimination intervention cannot be gainsaid. Successful class action lawsuits have involved rulings, settlements, or consent decrees under which employers are obliged to increase their representation of protected-class members. Furthermore, even the filing of a charge can alter an employer's behavior; O&G Spring and Wire's sudden increase in black hires after the EEOC's intervention is far from unique.[21] Finally, the threat of employment discrimination litigation inherent in the existence of the corpus of law certainly would appear to reduce employment discrimination and increase employer affirmative action efforts.

Indeed, even in the South in the 1960s, the scene of blacks' greatest relative progress provisionally attributed primarily to Jim Crow's demise and the promulgation of federal antidiscrimination policy, federal efforts presumably made a difference. Half the country's employment discrimination lawsuits in 1966–72 were filed in the South.[22] In particular, blacks' dramatic post-1965 increase in employment in South Carolina's textile firms—unmatched in any other state industry[23]—would appear to be the result of the EEOC's targeting southern textiles and conducting hearings on the industry in late 1966 and early 1967, as well as the sale of 5 percent of the industry's output to the federal government: "The Defense Department, which was in charge of monitoring textile affirmative action programs, was known to be relatively vigorous in pursuit of equal opportunity. Three large textile companies in North and South Carolina had government contracts withdrawn for a brief period in 1968 because of noncompliance with the [Executive] Order [11246]."[24] And because

20. Donohue and Heckman, "Continuous versus Episodic Change," p. 1606.

21. See subsection 4.2.3 above.

22. Donohue and Heckman, "Continuous versus Episodic Change," p. 1637.

23. Heckman and Payner, "Determining the Impact of Federal Antidiscrimination Policy," p. 158.

24. Ibid., p. 143.

textile mills are often monopsonists insulated from labor market competition, federal antidiscrimination efforts directed at them would be expected to have an especially strong impact, just as lawsuits against police and fire departments, which also have monopsony power because police officers and firefighters have few alternative job opportunities without switching occupations, have induced significant increases in blacks' employment.[25]

On the other hand, the major breakthroughs in black employment in South Carolina's textile firms were in fiscal years 1965 and 1966, that is, between July 1964 and June 1966[26]—before the EEOC hearings and Defense Department penalties. Blacks continued to experience gains thereafter, as further employee turnover allowed black workers to replace whites. Revised stereotyping followed in the wake of shifting employment patterns. Blacks formerly considered by whites to be untrainable and irresponsible were later judged to be more productive mill workers as a consequence of their "natural rhythm."[27]

Were the gains in black employment a response to passage of Title VII, which gave employers an excuse to violate long-standing norms and pursue a profit-maximizing strategy of hiring blacks, or a response to anticipated future lawsuits and federal enforcement? The balance tips in favor of the first explanation upon noting that textiles was both the only South Carolina industry with underrepresentation of blacks in 1960[28] and apparently the only industry to whose employment practices Jim Crow had specifically applied for almost fifty years:[29]

> That it shall be unlawful; for any person, firm or corporation engaged in the business of cotton textile manufacturing in this State to allow or permit operatives, help and labor of different races to labor and work together within the same room, or to use the same doors of entrance and exit at the same time, or . . . to use the same stairway and

25. Jerome McCristal Culp, "Federal Courts and the Enforcement of Title VII," *American Economic Review* 76: 2 (May 1986): 355–58. The extent to which litigation shifted these departments' policies essentially from discrimination to neutrality, rather than from neutrality to affirmative action, no doubt varies considerably from case to case.

26. Heckman and Payner, "Determining the Impact of Federal Antidiscrimination Policy," pp. 160–61.

27. Joan Hoffman, *Racial Discrimination and Economic Development* (Lexington, Mass.: D. C. Heath, 1975), p. 9.

28. In 1960, black men were not underrepresented in any South Carolina industries except textiles, and black women were not underrepresented in any industries except textiles and (the closely related industry) apparel manufacturing. Heckman and Payner, "Determining the Impact of Federal Antidiscrimination Policy," p. 158.

29. Epstein, *Forbidden Grounds,* pp. 246–47. All else equal, a Jim Crow law applying only to one industry would have maximal employment effects when applied to the largest. And South Carolina's textile industry accounted for 62 percent of the state's value added in manufacturing in 1963 (Hoffman, *Racial Discrimination and Economic Development*, p. 35)—and presumably similar proportions in earlier years.

windows at the same time, or to use at any time the same lavatories, toilets, drinking water buckets, pails, cups, dippers or glasses.[30]

There is no question that Title VII of the Civil Rights Act had substantial impact on southern labor markets in the decade after its passage. Its aftermath appears to be due primarily to the invalidation of southern segregation and promulgation of a federal standard by which Americans were expected to abide, rather than to federal government intervention, including employment discrimination lawsuits. The apparent minimal impact of Title VII regulation in later years in the South or in other regions of the country at any time supports this interpretation.

6.2 Effects of the Federal Contract Compliance Program

Studies of the OFCCP's impact have compared the race and sex composition of the work forces of similar contractors and noncontractors, focusing principally on differential growth rates in minority and female versus white and male employment.[31] The basic conclusion of this literature is that contractors have fostered significantly higher growth in the employment rates of protected-class members than noncontractors, especially when subject to compliance reviews, during which OFCCP equal opportunity specialists visit, audit employment policies and records, and negotiate greater efforts on behalf of protected-class members. The conclusions of the studies are quite consistent.[32]

A typical estimate of the OFCCP's effect on the annual increased share of employment for black males is that between 1974 and 1980, namely, 62/100ths of 1 percent for contractors not receiving a compliance review, 1.91 percent for those reviewed,[33] with a weighted average of 84/100ths of 1 percent. Corresponding gains for other minority men, white women, and black women were 1.69 percent, 0.37 percent, and 2.13 percent.[34] Thus, assume that a similar contractor and noncontractor each had work forces with the same percentage of black men. Suppose further that, at the end of ten years, 7 percent of the noncontractor's work force consisted of black men. Then the 84/100ths of 1 percent greater annual growth rate for contractors,

30. South Carolina Criminal Code, Sec. 45, as quoted in Epstein, *Forbidden Grounds,* pp. 246–47.

31. Thus, if, in a recession, an employer lays off only whites, stable black employment implies relative black gains.

32. See Jonathan S. Leonard, "The Impact of Affirmative Action Regulation and Equal Employment Law on Black Employment," *Journal of Economic Perspectives* 4: 4 (Fall 1990): 47–63.

33. Although compliance reviews were more likely to take place at large and growing firms, their incidence has not been systematically related to employment patterns by race and sex. Ibid., pp. 56–58.

34. See p. 453 in Jonathan S. Leonard, "The Impact of Affirmative Action on Employment," *Journal of Labor Economics* 2: 4 (October 1984): 439–63.

Table 6.2   Budget and Staffing of the
Office of Federal Contract Compliance Programs

| Fiscal year | Appropriation | | Staff |
	Current $ (000)	Constant $ (000)	
1979	42,940	59,146	1480
1980	53,053	64,385	1482
1981	49,680	54,653	1482
1982	43,150	44,715	1008
1983	43,815	43,991	979
1984	46,333	44,594	979
1985	46,630	43,336	964
1986	43,677	39,851	935
1987	47,191	41,541	910
1988	50,375	42,582	970
1989	51,863	41,825	970
1990	53,045	40,585	969
1991	52,585	38,609	918
1992	54,655	38,984	856

Sources: Unpublished data, Department of Labor, Office of Federal Contract Compliance Programs for current dollar fiscal year authorized budget and authorized full-time equivalent staffing; *Economic Report of the President, 1993*, table B-58, for consumer price index allowing transformation of current dollar budgets into constant (1982–84) dollar budgets.

equivalent to an 8.72 percent change over ten years, implies that black men would constitute 7.61 percent of the contractor's employees at the end of the ten-year period.[35] Therefore, if each had ten thousand employees, the noncontractor would employ 700 black men, and the contractor 761.

The OFCCP's impact was greater in the 1970s than in the 1980s. Before 1980, 10 percent growth in total establishment employment "could be expected to result in black male employment growth of 12 percent among non-contractors and 17 percent among contractors. After 1980, the comparable rates are 11 percent among non-contractors and 10 percent among contractors. The reversal for black females is even more marked."[36]

The OFCCP's budget and staffing levels are consistent with its attenuated effects in the 1980s. After peaking in (fiscal year) 1980, the office's budget declined by about 20 percent from 1980 to 1982, decreasing somewhat thereafter in constant dollars while generally increasing slightly in current dollars (table 6.2).[37] Staffing, almost 1,500 in 1979–81, was below 1,000 for most of

35. Translating 84/100ths of 1 percent into a ten-year shift involves taking 1.0084 to the tenth power. The result is 1.0872, indicating a ten-year growth rate of 8.72 percent. Multiplying 7 percent by 1.0872 yields 7.61 percent.

36. Leonard, "The Impact of Affirmative Action Regulation," p. 58.

37. Comparable data are not available before 1979 because the federal contract compliance effort was spread over several agencies.

the 1980s. The OFCCP's budget and staffing are roughly one-third of those of the EEOC, an order of magnitude roughly commensurate with the relative number of employees covered by both agencies' regulations: About 80 percent of private sector employees in the United States work for firms covered by Title VII (table 6.3), and 30 percent for federal contractors (table 5.1).

It is possible that the literature's contractor-noncontractor differences understate or overstate the contract compliance program's effect. Noncontractors may aggressively recruit protected-class members as part of a program to win government contracts. Thus, if the OFCCP increased protected-class members' representation in noncontractor work forces by 2 percent and in contractor work forces by 5 percent, the 3 percent contractor-noncontractor difference would understate program impact. On the other hand, if the least discriminating firms are thereby more efficient and underbid others to win contracts, then the OFCCP is simply rewarding rather than inducing nondiscriminatory behavior.[38]

I find neither of these points persuasive. First, by virtue of the goods and services they produce, some firms (e.g., defense manufacturers) are always government contractors, while others (e.g., specialty retail establishments) rarely, if ever, seek federal contracts. Furthermore, the movement between contractor and noncontractor status is bilateral: About 11 percent of 1974 contractors were noncontractors in 1980, and 27 percent of 1974 noncontractors were contractors in 1980.[39] Thus, anticipatory minority recruitment and hiring efforts by new contractors could be countered by relaxation of similar efforts by former contractors forgoing government business. Most important, firms have ample time to hire minorities and women in the face of an incipient contract award, and subsequent required affirmative action plan submissions.

Moreover, the conjunction of low product prices and nondiscriminatory behavior is unlikely, because the OFCCP's interpretation of nondiscrimination includes effective affirmative action, the achievement of which tends to involve higher costs from extra efforts in both recruitment and government compliance (see section 4.3.1), and perhaps inefficient employee hiring and allocation by demographics rather than qualifications. Indeed, a comparison of contractors and noncontractors revealed that "contractors had costs that were 6.5% greater than they would have been if they had been non-contractors. The average contractor had costs of nearly $395 million, so the average cost of complying with affirmative action for contractors in this sample was around $26 million in 1980."[40] Thus, because neither understatement nor overstatement of the OFCCP's effect seems plausible, the studies are probably on the mark.

The federal compliance program also appears to have promoted the occupa-

38. Butler and Heckman, "The Government's Impact," p. 251.

39. Leonard, "The Impact of Affirmative Action on Employment," p. 461.

40. Quote from p. 259 in Peter Griffin, "The Impact of Affirmative Action on Labor Demand: A Test of Some Implications of the LeChatelier Principle," *Review of Economics and Statistics* 74: 2

tional advancement of blacks within contractor establishments. In the middle and late 1970s, but not before, the representation of blacks in most occupations—including high-paying professional and managerial positions—increased at a greater rate among federal contractors than noncontractors.[41] Similar patterns obtained between 1966 and 1980 in the larger set of firms required to submit EEO-1 reports (see section 6.3).Consistent with this pattern of occupational advancement, "[m]inority male wages are higher relative to those of white males in cities and industries with a high proportion of employment in federal contractor establishments subject to affirmative action, although the effect is not always significant."[42]

The historical pattern of pay appears to be similar to that of employment, with striking relative black wage and earnings gains only in the South from the mid-1960s to the mid-1970s (see section 6.1) and relatively greater occupational advancement in contractor and EEO-1 reporting firms. Increased demand for minorities by federal contractors and firms required to file EEO-1 reports would tend to raise minority pay in these sectors, an effect reinforced by large firms' generally providing higher pay and fringe benefits than comparable smaller firms.[43] However, evaluating the *aggregate* effects of these programs on blacks' pay would involve both extricating the direct effect of the programs from all other determinants of pay and addressing the impact of the programs on the location of new establishments in areas with few minorities, minorities' incentives for skill acquisition, and the like.[44] Indeed, not only has relative pay not improved for blacks outside the South and since the mid-1970s, but researchers have documented the deterioration of black men's earnings relative to those of white men in the last two decades.[45]

6.3 Interpretation

Given that Title VII and the federal contract compliance program both appear to have had a positive impact on the employment of blacks (and, although less

---

(May 1992): 251–60. Because the EEO-1 data analyzed in this paper do not distinguish employees directly producing goods and services for sale from those involved in regulatory compliance, the greater contractor costs reflect to an unknown extent direct contractor compliance costs and differences in productivity across sectors. It is possible, although contrary to the discussion in this paper and that in section 5.3 above, that contractors' employees are as efficient as or more efficient than noncontractors', so Griffin's results would reflect the cost burden of employing personnel for regulatory compliance.

41. Leonard, "The Impact of Affirmative Action Regulation," pp. 52–54.

42. Ibid., pp. 53–54.

43. See Brown, Hamilton, and Medoff, *Employers Large and Small,* chaps. 4 and 5.

44. As noted in the introduction, an analysis of pay is outside the scope of this book.

45. See the summary article by Philip Moss and Chris Tilly, "A Turn for the Worse: Why Black Men's Labour Market Fortunes Have Declined in the United States," *Sage Race Relations Abstracts* 18: 1 (February 1993): 5–45, esp. 8–12.

Table 6.3　Distribution of Work Force by Size of Establishment

Size of establishment (employees)	Number of employees (millions)	Percent of total
1–10	13.86	15.1
10–19	10.13	11.1
20–99	26.83	29.3
100+	40.81	44.5
Total	91.63	100.0

Source: U.S. Department of Commerce, Bureau of the Census, *County Business Patterns, 1989* (published 1992), table 1b. (Excludes federal, state, and local government employees except those working in government-operated hospitals and liquor stores; railroad employees; and self-employed persons. Includes employees of private educational institutions.)

studied, on other minority groups and on white women), why do we observe the persistence of the unemployment rate differentials presented in tables 3.1– 3.3? How can we reconcile this seemingly contradictory evidence?

Three explanations can be dismissed directly: (1) the level of discrimination is increasing over time; (2) no significant employer discrimination or policies have adverse impact on protected-class members; and (3) the antidiscrimination programs are not covering much of the labor market.

First, the level of discrimination has probably been *decreasing* over time. Racist beliefs, inhospitable attitudes toward women, and disparities in the treatment of black and white testers in fair housing audit studies all have been declining.[46] Second, despite the apparent reduction in discrimination, the studies reported in chapter 3 suggest that substantial barriers are still present, particularly for blacks and Hispanics. Third, as table 6.3 shows, about 80 percent of private sector employees work in firms subject to Title VII coverage.[47]

A more plausible explanation is that other aspects of the labor market are neutralizing the impact of the antidiscrimination programs. The studies reviewed in the prior sections of this chapter have attempted to control for some of these. The Title VII effects were estimated as a residual after other labor market changes were taken into account. And by comparing similarly situated contractors and noncontractors at the same time, much else has been held constant.

46. Donohue and Siegelman, "The Changing Nature of Employment Discrimination Litigation," pp. 1001–2.

47. Data on firms with fifteen or more employees are not available. Table 6.3 indicates that about 85 percent of firms have ten or more employees, and about 75 percent twenty or more; hence, between 75 percent and 85 percent—perhaps 80 percent—have fifteen or more. A further complication is that the employers reported in table 6.3 and those required to file EEO-1 reports are not the same. Private employers other than educational institutions file EEO-1 reports. Table 6.3 excludes most public sector workers but includes those working in government hospitals and liquor stores; and it excludes railroad workers but includes employees of private educational institutions.

Nonetheless, still other factors may have increased black-white employment differentials. The decline in manufacturing, the deteriorating demand for unskilled labor within domestic industries, and the growing suburbanization of employment—the increasing proportion of suburban rather than urban jobs—all may have disproportionately constricted job opportunities for minorities. The suburbanization effect has been mitigated by the migration of blacks to the suburbs. Indeed, the ruinous condition of many inner cities reflects to a great extent the exodus of many successful blacks.[48]

Minority job seekers within the swelling "underclass"[49] may be particularly vulnerable to employer stereotyping like that noted at the end of section 3.1—even with a general reduction in discrimination. Moreover, minorities' ability to benefit from diminished prejudice against them is limited by the residential segregation that restricts access to whites' job information networks.

To the extent that antidiscrimination and affirmative action regulation has increased (or restrained the decline of) the pay of blacks, it has thereby both discouraged demand for now relatively more expensive black labor and encouraged blacks' labor force participation. At the same time, widening gaps in the pay between skilled and unskilled labor, the latter comprising operatives, laborers, and service workers with disproportionate minority representation (see table 6.4), would have counterbalancing effects.[50]

Participation in inner-city drug traffic and crime reduces minority employment for several reasons: The illegal activity shifts blacks and Hispanics away from legal jobs, thus reducing *measured* employment; swells the ranks of minorities with criminal records, thus increasing the number of them who would be summarily ruled out from serious consideration as job candidates and consequently denied employment opportunities; and discourages the establishment of inner-city businesses that might employ nearby minority residents.[51]

48. See William Julius Wilson, *The Truly Disadvantaged: The Inner City, the Underclass, and Public Policy* (Chicago: University of Chicago Press, 1987), esp. pp. 56–62, in which middle- and working-class blacks are described as social buffers who used to provide stable models for inner-city underclass youth.

49. Between 1970 and 1980 the number of people in the "underclass"—indicators for which are working-age male nonparticipants in the labor market, female-headed households with children, welfare recipients, and school dropouts—increased much faster than the number of individuals living in poverty. See Erol R. Ricketts and Ronald B. Mincy, "Growth of the Underclass," *Journal of Human Resources* 25: 1 (Winter 1990): 137–45.

50. The decline in the employment-population ratio between 1967 and 1987 is especially pronounced for less-educated and low-wage men and apparently reflects a withdrawal from the labor market in response to pay rates that failed even to keep pace with inflation. See Chinhui Juhn, "Decline of Male Labor Market Participation: The Role of Declining Market Opportunities," *Quarterly Journal of Economics* 107: 1 (February 1992): 79–121.

51. The employment effects of inner-city drug traffic and crime, contraction of the domestic manufacturing sector, declining demand for low-skilled labor, and increasing suburbanization of employment are considered in more detail in chapter 7.

Table 6.4   Representation of Minorities and Women

	Federal contractors	Firms filing EEO-1 reports	Experienced labor force
Occupational category	Minorities (%)		
Officials and managers	10.1	10.1	13.1
Professionals	13.5	13.0	15.6
Technicians	18.8	19.0	19.6
Sales workers	18.6	18.8	17.5
Office and clerical workers	24.2	23.1	21.7
Craft workers	17.0	17.5	18.5
Operatives	28.8	28.9	30.3
Laborers	36.1	37.2	31.8
Service workers	40.5	39.4	32.5
Total	22.2	22.5	21.8
	Women (%)		
Officials and managers	25.0	28.1	36.0
Professionals	37.8	48.0	53.4
Technicians	35.4	44.8	44.1
Sales workers	52.5	57.2	53.9
Office and clerical workers	82.5	83.4	77.2
Craft workers	8.8	10.6	7.5
Operatives	32.5	33.4	31.5
Laborers	33.4	34.4	16.4
Service workers	51.0	55.5	58.2
Total	40.9	46.1	45.7

Sources: 1990 contractor and EEO-1 unpublished data from U.S. Department of Labor, Office of Federal Contract Compliance Programs. 1990 Census unpublished labor force data from U.S. Department of Commerce, Bureau of the Census.

A greater proportion of blacks than whites residing in areas where drugs are commonly sold is not a sufficient condition for drug traffic to have intensified racial unemployment differences over time. The relative number of blacks living near drug markets must be increasing. That is, the presence of drug traffic in black neighborhoods may explain (in part) why the black unemployment rate exceeds that of whites. However, to explain *expanding* black-white unemployment differentials by the increase in drug traffic requires in addition that drug traffic be growing at a greater rate in black than in white neighborhoods.

Given the stability in black-white unemployment rate differentials, other factors would have to have had more effect at times when antidiscrimination enforcement was stronger in order to attribute a significant impact to antidiscrimination regulation. That is, if the increase in drug traffic had greater employment effects in the 1980s than in the 1970s and if antidiscrimination enforcement was weaker in the 1980s than in the 1970s,[52] then the racial un-

52. The EEOC and the OFCCP reduced staffing in the 1980s (see sections 6.1 and 6.2), and the OFCCP's impact was apparently weaker in the 1980s than in the 1970s (see section 6.2).

employment gap should have narrowed in the 1970s and widened in the 1980s. Its relative constancy throughout the twenty-year period suggests insignificant overall effects of antidiscrimination policy. Moreover, the pattern of low-skilled blacks' employment deterioration began in the 1970s (section 3.2), when the level of antidiscrimination enforcement was still on the upswing.

I believe that the most plausible reconciliation of the evidence is that the contractor-noncontractor differences primarily represent demographic shifts across these two employer categories rather than net economy-wide gains for minorities. Furthermore, aside from the concentrated employment effects in the South in the late sixties and early seventies apparently reflecting to a great extent, if not exclusively, passage of the Civil Rights Act of 1964 and its repeal of Jim Crow, rather than its enforcement efforts, Title VII has likely also pro-duced employment shifts rather than gains, although more subtly than in the case of contractors and noncontractors.

The shifting effect can be illustrated by imagining two similar firms in a racially mixed small town. Suppose Firm A becomes a federal contractor or, alternatively, is successfully sued under Title VII by a plaintiff alleging racial discrimination in hiring and is then required to increase its employment of blacks. In either case, Firm A initiates efforts to recruit blacks, and hires many black applicants. When Firm B later advertises job vacancies, the black appli-cants who would have responded are already employed at Firm A. Although Firm A employs significantly more blacks than Firm B, the overall black em-ployment rate remains the same.[53]

Because Title VII covers about 80 percent of the private sector labor force, how can Title VII's effects reflect a redistribution of employees? The noncov-ered sector consists only of firms with at most fourteen employees, and this sector is too small to supply minority workers to the rest of the economy and not likely to employ many minorities because its mostly white employers pre-sumably recruit through their largely white personal networks.

The answer lies in the intensity with which sectors of the labor market are regulated. Although the noncovered sector is limited to employers of fourteen or fewer, about 55 percent of the private sector labor market comprises firms employing no more than one hundred employees (table 6.3). Unless they are federal contractors subject to OFCCP affirmative action requirements, these firms are not required to file EEO-1 reports and consequently are not moni-tored systematically by any government agency.[54] Moreover, three-quarters of

53. This analysis can be extended with two-sector models in which employment and wage changes induced by these programs depend on labor demand and supply elasticities in each sector.

54. Employment discrimination lawsuits stem from two sources: EEOC review of employer EEO-1 reports, after which the EEOC can file Commissioner's Charges, even without a single complainant; and the more familiar individual complaints brought directly by private plaintiffs, perhaps with the assistance of the EEOC or a state Fair Employment Practice agency. Occasion-ally, Commissioner's Charges and class action lawsuits result from individual complaints.

the work force are with employers who are not federal contractors and there-fore have no affirmative action obligations. Thus, more than half the work force is to a great extent insulated from administrative review by the EEOC.[55]

In addition, the employment discrimination laws themselves provide em-ployers with incentives *not* to employ minorities—or women or older work-ers. How? To begin, especially in recent years, the likelihood of an applicant bringing a hiring discrimination lawsuit is much lower than that of a present or former employee filing an employment discrimination lawsuit on other grounds. According to the American Bar Foundation Employment Litigation Survey, between 1972 and 1987, only 19 percent of employment discrimi-nation lawsuits focused on hiring, 59 percent alleged discrimination in ter-mination, and the remaining 22 percent complained of discrimination in pay, promotion, assignment, and other employer policies.[56] With five applicants for each incumbent employee, the probability that an applicant will file a lawsuit is less than 5 percent of the probability that an employee will file one.[57] Con-sequently, assuming that employers' costs and damages are roughly the same for hiring and other classes of employment discrimination lawsuits, employers will, on average, be minimizing litigation expenses by not hiring protected-class workers.

In fact, on average, damages are probably relatively low in hiring cases, re-inforcing incentives to avoid hiring protected-class members and to risk law-suits from applicants rather than employees. Basic damages for hiring cases equal the difference between earnings if hired and income actually earned, most of which obtains from the plaintiff's period between jobs, particularly when the plaintiff's former and new job pay is roughly equal to that of the defendant employer. If the plaintiff is an active job seeker and/or begins job search while employed, this unemployment period may be quite short. In contrast, terminated employees begin a job search while unemployed, and their stigma of a recent involuntary termination is a major disadvantage in labor market competition. Thus, their unemployment period may be longer and damages greater than that of other applicants. Employees prevailing on

55. According to table 5.1, 47.0 percent of private sector employees and 36.4 percent of all employees worked in establishments filing EEO-1 reports. The 47.0 percent figure is close to table 6.3's 44.5 percent of private sector employees in firms of one hundred or more, excluding railroads and the self-employed. Estimates of the proportion of employees working for federal contractors cannot be derived from table 6.3, only from table 5.1.

56. Donohue and Siegelman, "The Changing Nature of Employment Discrimination Litiga-tion," p. 1015.

57. The ratio of hiring to other lawsuits is 19/81 = .23. If there are five times as many applicants as employees, then the result in the text follows from .23 divided by 5 being less than .05. The number of applicants per employee increases with employee turnover and the number of appli-cants per job vacancy. With 100 percent turnover, the annual number of applicants per job vacancy will equal the number of applicants per employee.

grounds of discrimination in pay (perhaps related to allegations of discrimination in promotion, assignment, or access to overtime) can be awarded back pay with interest. Perhaps most important, individual lawsuits by terminated or current employees invite former or present coworkers to assess their chances for successful litigation, perhaps as a class action. In contrast, the typical applicant acts alone, and does not influence a class of applicants.

The strategy of not hiring protected-class members would not appear to be rational for federal contractors, because systematic shortfalls of protected-class employees can attract the OFCCP's attention, and thereby endanger the retention and acquisition of federal contracts. Only when the proportion of sales accounted for by the federal government is small might this strategy be cost-minimizing.

To a lesser extent, noncontractors required to file EEO-1 reports that are monitored by the EEOC also would not be acting rationally if they were to avoid hiring minorities and women. However, even within the group of firms with one hundred or more employees, smaller employers face less risk by not hiring protected-class members. The EEOC is presumably most likely to investigate larger employers who have more jobs that could be filled by minorities and women.[58] Also, the smaller the employer, generally the smaller the number of hires within any time period. And EEOC economists and statisticians are well aware that, holding constant the availability percentage, statistically significant hiring disparities are more likely to obtain, the greater the total number of hires. Thus, with similar percentage shortfalls relative to availability, larger employers are more likely than smaller ones to have attendant statistically significant hiring disparities.

To minimize the risk that rejected applicants will sue, employers can pursue recruitment practices that do not attract protected-class members. As noted in chapters 2 and 3, the array of targeted recruitment practices available to employers gives them a great deal of control over the racial and ethnic composition of their applicants.

Employers also can choose to locate in areas where relatively few minorities live. A firm with an initial establishment in an area where minority availability was 30 percent might relocate or open a new site in an area with 5 percent minority availability. An illuminating project would involve investigating the pattern of minority availability in locations of new establishments over time. New plants established overseas and not covered by American regulation could be defined as being in areas with zero minority availability, whatever the presence of minorities in the external labor market. Of course, other factors, such as local wage levels and tax policy, would have to be taken into account in any analysis of employer location. A related study could compare the locations of

---

58. Recall that the OFCCP's compliance reviews focused on large firms. See section 6.2.

new establishments among the various classes of employer: federal contractors, noncontractors required to submit EEO-1 forms, noncontractors not required to submit EEO-1 forms, and small businesses not covered by Title VII. The hypothesis to be tested is that heavily regulated firms more susceptible to employment discrimination lawsuits would be more likely to locate in areas with low minority availability.[59] Less regulated and noncovered firms would experience little or no modification in regulatory burden with varying representation of minorities in their labor markets.

It is also possible, although not as plausible as the effects so far discussed, that firms may shift to less labor-intensive methods of production in an attempt to reduce their work forces below the one-hundred-employee trigger for submission of EEO-1 reports or even the fifteen-employee Title VII coverage threshold. In any case, by decreasing the required number of employees, hires, and applicants and the concomitant exposure to employment discrimination litigation (and other regulation), production processes with few workers and expensive machinery have become relatively more attractive than those with many workers and cheaper machinery.

All these considerations suggest that the representation of minorities and women should be greatest for federal contractors, relatively high for firms required to file EEO-1 reports, and lowest for firms whose size is below EEO-1 reporting requirements. Unfortunately, it is difficult to obtain data to test this proposition, principally because of the noncomparability of industry and occupations across these employer categories. For example, relative to the private sector labor market excluding education, firms filing EEO-1 reports are more likely to comprise manufacturing establishments, and less likely to include those in wholesale and retail trade.[60]

More important, the varying mix of occupations required for the three groups of employers renders somewhat meaningless a comparison of minority and female representation among all employees. For example, the representation of women among craft workers is far below that among clericals. If, hypothetically, employers of craft workers are much more likely than employers

59. This point is supported in Richard A. Posner, "The Efficiency and Efficacy of Title VII," *University of Pennsylvania Law Review* 136: 2 (December 1987): 513–21; p. 519, n. 27, with evidence from *Terry Properties, Inc. v. Standard Oil Co.*, 799 F. 2d 1523, 1527, that the defendant desired to "build its plant in a city with a minority population no greater than 35% of the total population, allegedly because it had previously experienced difficulty meeting affirmative action goals in communities with proportionately larger minority populations."

60. Although the number of employees working in establishments required to file EEO-1 reports constitutes roughly 47 percent of the total in the comparable private sector labor market, only 25 percent of employees in wholesale and retail trade, but more than 60 percent of employees in manufacturing, work in firms subject to EEO-1 reporting requirements. See *Job Patterns for Minorities and Women in Private Industry—1989* (Washington: U.S. Equal Employment Opportunity Commission, 1990).

of clericals to be federal contractors, then the differing male-female composition of the two occupations would be reflected in contractor-noncontractor comparisons. At the same time, the male-female composition of craft or clerical workers among contractor and noncontractor employers may not differ significantly.

Comparisons within broad occupational categories reduce but do not eliminate the noncomparability because of remaining heterogeneity within them. Employers filing EEO-1 reports not only vary in their classification schemes but, in particular, may upgrade the occupational categories of minorities and women to protect themselves from assignment and promotion discrimination investigations based on theories that minorities and women are shunted into dead-end jobs or, for other reasons, not promoted. For the same reason, employers may prefer hiring highly skilled to less skilled protected-class members.[61] Furthermore, because minorities have relatively high unemployment rates, their representation in the experienced labor force—including employed persons and the unemployed who have held a job in the last five years (from which their occupational category is determined)—will be greater than that among the employed.

Finally, the locations of contractors and firms filing EEO-1 reports may not be representative of those of the entire labor market, and their minority and—to a much lesser extent—female availability correspondingly higher or lower. To take a simple example, if all reporting firms are found—perhaps because they seek to reduce their regulatory burden by setting up establishments in areas with few minorities—in labor markets with 10 percent minority availability, and heavily recruit minorities therein, they may achieve a work force that is 15 percent minority, while in the nonreporting firms in the same area only 5 percent of the work force is minority. At the same time, in other labor markets, nonreporting firms disproportionately located in big cities or other areas with high minority availability may have a work force that is 35 percent minority. Assuming half the employees of nonreporting firms are in the same labor markets as those working for reporting firms yields a minority representation in all nonreporting firms of 20 percent (the simple average of 5 percent and 35 percent). The contrast between 20 percent minorities in nonreporting firms and 15 percent in reporting firms certainly provides no evidence of the reporting firms' aggressive minority recruitment, and falsely appears to contradict it.

These objections notwithstanding, table 6.4 provides mild support for the greater representation of minorities in heavily regulated firms: In 1990, the proportions of minorities and women among 23.6 million federal contractor

---

61. Finis Welch, "Affirmative Action and Its Enforcement," *American Economic Review* 71: 2 (May 1981): 127–33.

employees are 22.2 percent and 40.9 percent; among 36.2 million employees in firms filing EEO-1 reports including these contractors, 22.5 percent and 46.1 percent; and among the entire experienced civilian labor force, 21.8 percent and 45.7 percent. Because these groups overlap, the differences are greater than table 6.4 suggests: Subtracting reporting firms from the entire labor force yields a minority representation of only 21.5 percent, and because this includes the unemployed, it still overstates the minority representation among employees working in firms not required to file EEO-1 reports.

On the other hand, the table 6.4 breakdowns by occupation do not support the proposition that minorities and women are likely to be well represented in higher-paying jobs in contractor and other reporting firms. Subtracting public sector managers and teachers from the labor force does not alter this result: The most dramatic change, after removing teachers from the category of female professionals, reduces the female representation among labor force professionals to 47.1 percent, only slightly below that among reporting firms and still well above that for contractors.[62] It may be that minority and female professionals are highly represented among the self-employed, and that minority and female managers are disproportionately found in nonreporting workplaces such as small retail establishments. Aside from the manifold issues of data and interpretation, the patterns in table 6.4 may reflect "glass ceilings," jobs at levels dominated by white males and into which minorities and women often fail to be promoted because of intentional or unintentional discrimination for any of the reasons discussed in chapter 3.

Comparing the same category of establishments over time will hold constant many of the factors interfering with assessment of the extent to which heavily regulated firms are more likely to employ minorities and women. Indeed, time series evidence indicates that, especially in the higher-paying occupations, blacks' representation in covered or EEOC-reporting employers (i.e., those filing EEO-1 reports) increased dramatically between 1966 and 1980: "Black men were almost 10 percent less likely than white men to work in covered firms in 1966. By 1980, they were 25 percent more likely to work in EEOC-reporting firms. Compared with the 48 percent in 1966, fully 60 percent of all black men worked in covered firms by 1980." Furthermore, "48 percent of black women were in covered employment in 1966, but that figure reached 75 percent by 1980. Black females changed from being 10 percent less likely (than white men) to work in covered firms in 1966 to more than 50 percent more likely in 1980." And "[b]lack [male] managers and profes-

---

62. With the same adjustment, minority professionals' representation in the labor force decreased from 15.6 percent to 15.5 percent. Removing public administration and education managers from the officials and managers category reduced female labor market representation from 36.0 percent to 35.1 percent, and minority representation from 13.1 percent to 12.7 percent.

sionals [also including technicians] were half as likely as white [male] managers and professionals to work in covered firms in 1966. By 1980, black [male] managers and professionals were equally likely to be found in covered firms." Finally, "black women managers represent an even more dramatic relocation of employment. From 40 percent less likely [than white males] to work in covered firms, black women were 50 percent more likely to work in EEOC-covered jobs by 1980." The corresponding changes for black women in the professional and technical category were more than 25 percent less likely in 1966, and almost 20 percent more likely in 1980.[63] During this period of striking sectoral shifts, the aggregate relative black unemployment rate did not improve (see tables 3.2 and 3.3).

The salient conclusion of this section, that the enforcement of the antidiscrimination and affirmative action regulations has had no significant effect on aggregate minority employment, should be interpreted provisionally: It is impossible to prove the nonexistence of an effect. It is conceivable that future research, perhaps using 1990 Census data to study the impact during the 1980s of factors such as the decline in domestic manufacturing, deteriorating opportunities for low-skilled labor, suburbanization of employment, and drug traffic and crime, will establish that economy-wide minority employment is higher than it would have been in the absence of the employment discrimination laws. Nonetheless, it certainly appears that—apart from blacks' employment gains accompanying desegregation in the South in 1965–75—the laws have had negligible aggregate employment effects: Increased employment by federal contractors and large firms covered by Title VII in part has reduced the minorities available to less heavily regulated employers. Furthermore, the regulations have provided incentives for employers to avoid hiring members of protected classes, a goal easy to achieve, given the manifold possibilities for targeted recruitment as well as the long-run option of locating in areas with few minorities. Finally, firms' word-of-mouth recruitment and initial screening criteria lie to a great extent outside the ambit of federal regulation.

6.4 Private Policy

Even though policy discussions are almost always limited to proposals arguing for or against government intervention, a set of *private* policy alternatives is also available to participants in various markets. Thus, protected-class job seekers, their potential employers, and even sympathetic citizens can respond to the labor market environment.

The combination of ethnic stratification of social networks and the prominence of word-of-mouth recruitment bodes ill for ethnic groups with low rates of entrepreneurship. Thus, until blacks, Hispanics, and American Indians are

---

63. Smith and Welch, "Black Economic Progress after Myrdal," p. 554.

further established in their own businesses, minority job seekers other than some Asian-Americans generally will have relative difficulty finding work because of their less fruitful word-of-mouth networks. Minority job seekers must be prepared to look for work more intensively than whites, and to realize that their chances of finding work are much better with affirmative action–oriented large firms, particularly federal contractors, and with various levels of government.

The rationale for this suggested targeted job search is not based only on these sectors being more heavily regulated than small, private employers. Large firms are likely to use recruitment methods that widely publicize job opportunities and that minorities can discover as easily as whites. In contrast, small firms can fill many of their job openings through their limited word-of-mouth networks.

An analogy to renting an apartment is apposite: Even without newspaper advertisements, minority renters are well advised to search large apartment buildings—not only because these are prime targets for fair housing enforcement, but also because their frequent vacancies cannot be filled through the personal networks of (presumably white) unit owners or building managers. In contrast, whites renting rooms in their homes are usually not strictly regulated and can often fill vacancies through personal referrals. Minority renters seeking rooms in white neighborhoods would suffer several disadvantages: lack of knowledge of available rooms, outright racial discrimination, and rejection that might be perceived as discrimination but which in fact reflects the desire of owners to restrict potential tenants to those known personally, referred by friends, or culturally quite similar to themselves.[64]

Employers can try to minimize the likelihood of recruitment and hiring discrimination lawsuits by using recruitment methods, such as advertisements in major metropolitan daily newspapers, that have no disparate impact on protected-class members. In addition, keeping complete records can often deflect EEOC or other investigations, let alone lawsuits. Even a firm with a poor statistical hiring record may be relatively immune from discrimination allegations if it can demonstrate that its applicants were generated via recruitment methods that do not adversely affect any demographic group; that protected-class applicants were treated like similar white male applicants, in particular, rejected for valid nondiscriminatory reasons; or that including protected-class members and others who rejected offers of employment alters any apparently suspicious statistical hiring patterns.

Finally, concerned citizens can boycott the products of firms they believe are discriminating against certain groups. Boycotts have more potential impact

---

64. The point (and the example) is similar to that of the efficacy of walk-ins searching for jobs in large rather than small firms (subsection 2.2.2).

against firms whose products are purchased by consumers rather than used as intermediate components in other firms' production. Although boycotts of retail employers were a small part of the late 1950s and early 1960s civil rights movement, they were occasionally very effective.[65]

6.5 Public Policy

Although one of the conclusions in section 5.3 is that no antidiscrimination regulation appears to be Pareto-superior, policies will approach Pareto-superiority if the gains to some individuals strongly outweigh the losses to others. The simple promulgation of the Civil Rights Act of 1964 including its prohibition of Jim Crow provides an excellent example of "near-Pareto-superiority," a result obtained when a policy's gains to some are much greater than its losses to others.[66]

Theoretically, only white workers who now had to compete with blacks on a much more level playing field than before suffered major losses when the Civil Rights Act was passed. No reasonable equity argument can be offered to maintain segregation on behalf of southern white workers, who experienced no historical discrimination and, indeed, benefited from Jim Crow.

Another class of losers from desegregation were black hoteliers, restaurateurs, and others who once had a protected market, but after Jim Crow's repeal, faced much more competition as their black customers were able to patronize white establishments heretofore off-limits to them.[67] It seems reasonable to place these concerns after those of black labor force participants for at least three reasons. First, black employees far outnumber black entrepreneurs. Second, even after Jim Crow's demise, black customers could still patronize black businesses. Third, the effect on black business owners can be

65. For a history of the civil rights movement, see Ralph David Abernathy, *And the Walls Came Tumbling Down* (New York: Harper and Row, 1989), David J. Garrow, *Bearing the Cross: Martin Luther King, Jr., and the Southern Christian Leadership Conference* (New York: Morrow, 1986), and Aldon D. Morris, *The Origins of the Civil Rights Movement* (New York: Free Press, 1984). For examples of successful boycotts against employers, see Hannah Lees, "Boycott in Philadelphia," chap. 37, pp. 231–36, in Alan F. Westin, ed., *Freedom Now! The Civil Rights Struggle in America* (New York: Basic Books, 1964).

66. As noted in section 5.3, a Pareto-superior policy has no losers. Further, those opposed to government intervention—for which interpersonal comparisons can be a justification—would object to comparing gainers and losers to determine near-Pareto-superiority, always a subjective exercise. For example, a small sum of money transferred from a millionaire to a pauper would appear to be near-Pareto-superior, but not if the millionaire is a miser incurring a psychic loss, and certainly not if the pauper is an ascetic eschewing wealth.

67. A similar problem faces historically black colleges. Their top prospective students, who would have enrolled a generation ago, are now welcomed and often heavily recruited by other schools. Unlike southern white-owned restaurants and hotels, many colleges now recruiting blacks were not restricted by law from doing so in the past.

attributed narrowly to certain public accommodations provisions, which can in principle be viewed differently from the employment issues addressed by the Civil Rights Act of 1964.

Furthermore, although most of the empirical results on the effects of antidiscrimination policy can be interpreted as shifting workers across classes of employers, the one clear exception is blacks' dramatic improvement in the South in the late 1960s and early 1970s. As discussed in the prior section, part, perhaps virtually all, of these gains reflect desegregation.

Two final arguments support the repeal of Jim Crow. First, government administrative costs were reduced when monitoring segregation was no longer necessary. Second, both libertarian and equal-treatment considerations clearly support repeal of forced segregation.

The apparent lack of a strong effect of antidiscrimination and affirmative action regulation on aggregate minority employment other than that attributed to Jim Crow's repeal and Title VII's promulgation—in conjunction with limited information on other program effects and costs—precludes a comparable strong policy recommendation concerning current enforcement of Title VII or the federal contract compliance program. Indeed, the only clear-cut policy option based on the previous discussion is that the OFCCP's Eight Factors and overly strict underutilization definition should be jettisoned in favor of an availability analysis consonant with the methods of the EEOC, the courts, and the disciplines of economics and statistics (see section 4.3).

The lone study of the effect of the OFCCP on employers' costs concludes that contractors have 6.5 percent higher costs than comparable noncontractors (section 6.2), an amount equivalent to $40 billion annually.[68] Neither comparable estimates of the impact of EEOC regulation nor overall administrative costs (section 5.5) have been similarly calculated, although the roughly $210 million and $55 million annual budgets of the EEOC and OFCCP (tables 6.1 and 6.2) clearly provide floors for program administrative expenses. Additionally, direct litigation and, more speculatively, employers' efforts to avoid it, each has been estimated to cost about $100 million per year.[69] Thus, some will reserve judgment on these programs pending further analyses of costs and benefits, others will support or reject them in whole or in part on the basis of the theoretical arguments in chapter 5, and still others, given the conclusion of

68. The $40 billion amount is the approximate product of: the 6.5 percent contractor-noncontractor cost difference, the $2 trillion U.S. private sector payroll (U.S. Department of Commerce, Bureau of the Census, *County Business Patterns, 1989,* table 1b), and the 30 percent share of the private sector work force employed by federal contractors (table 5.1 above). See notes to tables 5.1 and 6.3 for precise definitions of the labor forces on which these data are based.

69. See p. 545 in John J. Donohue III, "Further Thoughts on Employment Discrimination Legislation: A Reply to Judge Posner," *University of Pennsylvania Law Review* 136: 2 (December 1987): 523–51.

section 6.3 in conjunction with these apparent employer costs,[70] will recommend a sharp reduction in the level, if not outright elimination, of current antidiscrimination and affirmative action enforcement.

Whatever one's views on these issues, several levers are available to effect policy shifts. Lawyers and lobbyists representing employers who wish to pursue, say, word-of-mouth recruitment without fear of violating antidiscrimination regulations can argue to courts that word-of-mouth recruitment meets business necessity criteria or is a passive employer (i.e., employee-generated) policy for which employers cannot be held responsible. Alternatively, employers can lobby Congress to raise the limit of Title VII noncoverage to a level above fifteen employees in order to exempt more small employers likely to rely heavily on word of mouth. Citizens wishing to limit personal referrals can take opposite positions. Those with intermediate views on the subject might propose emphasizing evidence on employer motives for word-of-mouth recruitment.

The significant impact of the federal contract compliance program on contractors' employment of minorities and women raises another question: Suppose these requirements were extended to all employers. Wouldn't we then have a powerful comprehensive antidiscrimination program that would considerably ameliorate the condition of blacks and other minorities? This question can be addressed under two enforcement scenarios: current OFCCP regulations, under which the representation of protected-class members must equal availability, and an alternative system preferred by most economists and statisticians and largely accepted by the EEOC and the courts, under which the representation of protected-class members must lie within two to three standard deviations of availability.

If the OFCCP regulations were universally mandated, employer demand for minorities and women would increase sharply and be reflected in protected-class members' increased pay and employment. Some occupational upgrading might obtain as well: To increase the number of black employees in upper-level job groups, black high school graduates might be hired into jobs requiring a college degree and then later required to do less than the job originally demanded.

These policies would increase the resentment, not to mention the unemployment, of whites and males. Complaints that they were passed over on grounds of race or sex, occasionally heard today but, in light of tables 3.1–3.3, difficult to accept as common, would become widespread. Some of the externalities introduced in section 5.3 would come into play. In particular, racial polarity

---

70. The increase in employer costs—and ultimately in product prices—is crucial: The $40 billion OFCCP-generated employer costs allocated over more than 200 million Americans equal roughly $200 per capita per year. The other administrative costs quantified in the text sum to only about $2 per capita per year.

would probably increase, and the achievements of minorities would be deemed a result of affirmative action rather than of competence and therefore downgraded in the eyes of those evaluating applicants.

Employers would try to avoid or to reduce their exposure to antidiscrimination regulation by moving to areas with few minorities, substituting capital for labor, establishing organizations with networks of individual subcontractors rather than employees, relying on temporary help agency referrals, moving offshore, or going out of business entirely. These private policies would reduce the overall number of jobs, and, by reducing the pie to be divided, conceivably could reduce the number of jobs for minorities and women below the level that would obtain in the absence of the regulations.

On the other hand, all these effects would be mitigated if the EEOC methodology were adopted. Suppose an employer is hiring into a job in a geographic area where the relevant black availability is 20 percent. Even if the employer should hire zero blacks, seventeen total hires are required before a statistical significance level equal to two standard deviations is present, and thirty total hires before three standard deviations is reached.[71] Thus, with this methodology, small and many medium-sized firms would be immune to class action lawsuits.

In general, the stricter the statistical criterion, the greater the rate of employee turnover, and the longer the period for which hires are to be tabulated, then the smaller the firm size below which employers can hire zero blacks without violating the regulation. For example, take a two-standard-deviation criterion, a three-year period of scrutiny, and 50 percent employee turnover. Assuming 20 percent black availability, with the two-standard-deviation criterion, firms with seventeen or more hires would be liable for a class action lawsuit with zero black hires. Seventeen hires in three years equals five and two-thirds hires per year. With 50 percent turnover, this is a firm with eleven and one-third, or, rounding, only twelve incumbent employees. Thus, the combination of these criteria (in areas with at least 20 percent black availability) would apply Title VII to employers of twelve—below the present fifteen-employee coverage threshold.

On the other hand, continue to assume 20 percent black availability, but change two standard deviations to three, 50 percent annual turnover to 10 percent, and a three-year time frame to one year. Firms with twenty-nine or fewer hires would not be liable for a class action lawsuit even with zero black hires. With 10 percent annual turnover and a time frame of only one year, twenty-nine hires for one year implies a firm of 290 employees. Thus, with this combina-

---

71. The probability of hiring seventeen consecutive nonblacks is .8 to the seventeenth power or .0225, just below .0228, which corresponds to two standard deviations. The probability of hiring thirty consecutive nonblacks is .8 to the thirtieth power or .0012, just below .0013, which corresponds to three standard deviations.

tion, even medium-sized firms with 290 or fewer employees would be exempt from Title VII (in areas with no more than 20 percent black availability).

Thus, this basic methodology is flexible enough to accommodate various doses of antidiscrimination regulation. Employee turnover is to a great extent under the employer's control, but the time frame and the choice of two or three standard deviations (or any other statistical criterion) would be up to Congress or the administration. The first example discussed above involves regulation of a firm below even Title VII's fifteen-employee limit, while the second would exclude a great number of firms now required to file EEO-1 reports.

The regulations would also have to address startup companies. Many small firms are founded with an owner or two, their coworkers at a former job, and some family members or friends. If these initial employees are considered to be hires, some owners might find that instead of working with those they know well and reaping advantages similar to those obtaining from word-of-mouth recruitment, they would be required to satisfy the statistical regulations by hiring minority employees previously unknown to them.

Furthermore, the stricter the regulations, the greater the incentives for employers to evade them. In particular, the proposed shift of focus from employees to hires provides incentives for employers to alter their hiring strategy. Hiring of whites and men might be increased at times when some protected-class members were hired, or when total hires were relatively small because employers could then accommodate more white male hires without violating the law's statistical hiring criteria. Unfortunately, hiring these white men (or others) at times they are not needed in response to antidiscrimination regulation is an inefficient labor-hoarding strategy.

Similarly, refraining from hiring additional employees because of the fear that new hires might include a white man who would push the recent hiring pattern to the illegal side of the statistical line imposes other costs such as turning away business, having current employees work overtime, and increasing output by the relatively inefficient policy of buying additional machinery instead of hiring labor.

The limits of even a greatly expanded antidiscrimination effort should now be apparent. With any reasonable statistical criterion, many small firms will be exempt. With even an OFCCP-like criterion of parity, some, although fewer, firms still will not be covered. For example, if 20 percent black availability means that 20 percent of a firm's employees must be black, five employees are necessary before one black among them would be required. Thus, firms of one to four employees will still lie outside the ambit of antidiscrimination regulation if they are in areas of no more than 20 percent black availability. And the employer avoidant behavior discussed previously will increase with stricter regulation. For example, under the parity criterion and with 20 percent minority availability, a small group of people from a large corporation wishing to go out on their own would be aware that with five or more employees at least one minority group member—whom they might not even know—would be required. Two or more firms, subcontracting arrangements, or a network of sole proprietorships then become relatively more attractive than a firm large enough to be subject to regulation.

What if all antidiscrimination regulation were repealed? Incentives to hire protected-class members and to avoid hiring them would both disappear. So would all the externalities and indirect effects discussed in chapter 5. Blacks and others would still suffer the affirmative action stigma from the years in which these laws were in force, even though they could no longer directly benefit from them in specific job competition. Minorities and women would have no government protection from discrimination. Litigation victories for protected-class members would be relegated to history.

One presumes that protected-class members would be worse off, but the arguments in this chapter render this plausible supposition ambiguous. Indeed, if the lack of regulation increased economic activity, protected-class members might have a reduced share of a greater economic pie that could represent either a larger or smaller slice than before. Deregulation would also eliminate employers' perverse incentives to avoid hiring minorities and women and allow private employers to allocate more resources to expanding production—and the number of jobs. The saving in public administrative costs would permit government spending that could have a more salubrious effect on minority and female labor market status than the present nexus of antidiscrimination and affirmative action regulations. Similar considerations obtain for stronger regulation, which would tend to increase the share of jobs held by minorities but decrease the total number of jobs in the economy. Minority workers would thus have a larger share of a smaller pie, the net effect of which again is not clear.

The persistence of the racial unemployment differentials presented in tables 3.1, 3.2, and 3.3 and the discussion of this chapter suggest that present antidiscrimination and affirmative action regulation has far fewer *economy-wide* effects than its proponents hope or its detractors fear. Furthermore, removing or strengthening antidiscrimination regulation probably would not substantially affect the overall employment status of protected classes. Thus, to improve minority employment prospects, policies other than antidiscrimination regulation must be considered. These are the subject of the next chapter.

CHAPTER SEVEN

Minority Employment Opportunities

The major conclusion of the previous chapter is that, apart from repealing Jim Crow, antidiscrimination and affirmative action laws and regulations seemingly have had no significant impact on aggregate minority employment: Their enforcement apparently redistributes minorities across categories of employers. Moreover, firms' recruitment practices and initial screening criteria limit the potential impact of alternative policies. Thus, other avenues must be explored to expand minority employment opportunities.

Section 7.1 is an overview of conventional recommendations to reduce unemployment, and section 7.2 is a discussion of issues primarily affecting inner-city minorities, especially young blacks. Of course, because minorities are disproportionately represented among the unemployed, even policies affecting overall employment are of particular importance to minority job seekers. Finally, section 7.3 focuses on improving minorities' job-seeking networks by increasing the rate of minority business formation, and providing informal short-term employment opportunities.

7.1 Conventional Employment Policies

A healthy economy growing at a sufficient rate to provide jobs for all—including new entrants and reentrants [1] to the labor force—is a boon for all job seekers: A rising tide lifts all boats. In particular, the employment of young men, especially blacks, is quite sensitive to local labor market conditions: When metropolitan unemployment rates fall, the unemployment rates of young black

---

1. New entrants are those who have never before held a job or sought work for pay. Reentrants are those who return to the labor force after a period of not being interested in holding a job; at some point prior to that period, they either held a paying job or sought to do so.

men fall disproportionately more.[2] Consistent with this observation, firms having difficulty filling vacancies recruit workers aggressively or relax their hiring standards. Energetic and creative outreach may include minority workers who are outside the ambit of usual recruitment practices. And moderating initial screening criteria may allow minority workers to be considered seriously for positions for which they ordinarily would be summarily rejected.[3]

Both macroeconomic and microeconomic policies can be enlisted to increase the number of jobs. Macroeconomic levers to enhance economic growth and to reduce unemployment and inflation include fiscal policy—government spending and taxation—and monetary policy—controlling the money supply to influence interest rates and the general level of prices. Economists vary in their prescriptions: Some prefer to establish long-term ground rules, emphasizing stability; while others opt to fine-tune the economy, stressing flexibility.

In contrast, microeconomics examines the behavior of individual consumers, producers, and workers. Labor economics comprises the subset of microeconomic analysis focusing on employers, workers, and job seekers.

Employment can be increased by reducing employers' labor costs or by increasing individuals' incentives to work; many policy options can be classified into one of these categories. Some policies that significantly affect employment were designed to address other issues. For example, minimum wage regulations are often viewed as means to assure adequate pay for the working poor. Yet by raising the cost of employing low-wage labor, minimum wage laws induce employers to automate processes, to locate plants in other countries where pay is lower, or to alter production methods so that a few skilled workers replace many unskilled. Less obviously, some firms that might have employed low-wage labor cannot operate profitably with minimum wages in effect and therefore are never established.[4]

Similarly, occupational licensing requirements can drastically reduce individuals' work opportunities by making illegal such unlicensed activities as using cars as cabs or renting trucks to move furniture. Arguments for licensing stress increasing public safety and assuring customers that those in various occupations are somewhat experienced and competent. These benefits must be

2. Richard B. Freeman, "Employment and Earnings of Disadvantaged Young Men in a Labor Shortage Economy," pp. 103–21 in Christopher Jencks and Paul E. Peterson, eds., *The Urban Underclass* (Washington: Brookings Institution, 1991).

3. Analogously, in nonexclusive hiring halls, contractors can request either specific union members or referrals from the union's out-of-work list. In boom markets, when the best reputed workers are likely to be fully employed, contractors will have to seek less skilled or less experienced workers from the out-of-work list.

4. See also the discussion of minimum wages in section 5.1, esp. note 4.

balanced against the constriction of employment opportunities—as well as the higher prices—that result when suppliers of services are restricted.[5]

In general, regulations influence economic growth and the number and type of jobs. To comply with regulations, firms must use resources that instead could be allocated to the production of goods and services for sale. Thus, rather than processing invoices, clerks will be compiling data for government-mandated reports. And rather than spending money to improve their plants, firms will have to purchase equipment required by government standards of safety, access for disabled persons, or environmental quality. In the long run, lower investment in plant and equipment implies reduced economic growth and fewer future jobs. In the short run, jobs lost by those directly involved in production become jobs gained by regulators and private sector personnel specializing in regulatory compliance. Citizens will differ on whether the benefits of these regulatory programs are worth their costs.

Transfer payments, from such programs as welfare and unemployment insurance, affect work incentives. Many of these programs have implicit tax rates in the sense that program payments are reduced when participants earn income. To take an oversimplistic but illustrative example, a welfare recipient of $3,000 annually who forfeits these payments upon taking a $10,000 per year job thus faces an implicit tax rate on earnings of 30 percent in addition to the explicit payroll taxes. Transfer payments' work disincentives must be considered along with their more obvious provision of income support. Because these programs modify the effective rate of pay employees receive, labor supply functions can measure their impact on labor force participation and hours of work.[6]

In general, lowering taxes reduces employers' labor costs and increases employees' take-home pay. Thus, expanding the Earned Income Tax Credit or otherwise cutting income taxes for employees or employers will increase job creation—but at the cost of reduced tax revenues that will inhibit funding of government programs. Subsidizing employment involves similar trade-offs. Until 1986, the Targeted Jobs Tax Credit allowed employers an income tax credit of up to $3,000 and $1,500 in the first and second years of employment for certain categories of workers—such as eighteen- to twenty-four-year-olds or Vietnam veterans—who were from economically disadvantaged (low-income) families.[7]

---

5. See Milton Friedman, *Capitalism and Freedom* (Chicago: University of Chicago Press, 1962), chap. 9, "Occupational Licensure," esp. pp. 137–49.

6. See John Pencavel, "Labor Supply of Men: A Survey," chap. 1, pp. 4–102, and Mark R. Killingsworth and James J. Heckman, "Female Labor Supply: A Survey," chap. 2, pp. 103–204, in Ashenfelter and Layard, eds., *Handbook of Labor Economics.*

7. For discussion of subsidized employment, see Robert Haveman and John L. Palmer, eds., *Jobs for Disadvantaged Workers: The Economics of Employment Subsidies* (Washington: Brookings

Implementation of targeted wage subsidy programs can have unforeseen effects. In an experiment in Dayton, Ohio, workers with vouchers indicating eligibility for generous wage subsidies, and thereby identified as disadvantaged workers, suffered reduced probabilities of receiving job offers. Vouchers presumably had a stigmatizing effect on job seekers.[8]

Enterprise zones are areas in which employers are free from some taxes or regulatory requirements. Exemptions from generally higher federal taxes provide much greater incentives for business formation than do exemptions only from state and local taxes. Yet even differentials in state and local taxes appear to attract industry.[9] Potentially larger federal tax exemptions could have much greater effects.

The discussion in section 3.2 suggests that white-owned firms in enterprise zones within minority neighborhoods might employ a percentage of minorities significantly below the corresponding minority representation in the local labor market. However, even if enterprise zones attracted white businesses that employed only whites, opportunities for minorities would still increase because of the growing total of jobs and the withdrawal of whites employed in enterprise zones from competition for other jobs in which minority workers would be interested. Directly regulating the minority composition of employees at these firms involves the trade-off noted in section 6.5: The stricter the regulation, the greater the proportion of minorities among employees, but the weaker the incentive for employers to establish jobs. The combination of a larger share of a smaller total of jobs can either increase or decrease the number of jobs for minorities.

Using the federal government as an employer of last resort or requiring welfare recipients to work involves a multitude of issues: How do taxpayers value the work produced as compared with spending on other government programs or on private sector consumption expenditures and savings that could have been realized had taxes not been collected to fund government jobs? Timing these programs is also tricky, especially given lags in legislation, funding, and implementation. A program designed to counter a recession may not take effect until a recovery has started. Job-creation programs designed for recessions

---

Institution, 1982), and Robert Eisner, "Employer Approaches to Reducing Unemployment," chap. 3, pp. 59–80, in D. Lee Bawden and Felicity Skidmore, eds., *Rethinking Employment Policy* (Washington: Urban Institute Press, 1989).

8. Gary Burtless, "Are Targeted Wage Subsidies Harmful? Evidence from a Wage Voucher Experiment," *Industrial and Labor Relations Review* 39: 1 (October 1985): 105–14.

9. James A. Papke and Leslie E. Papke, "Measuring Differential State-Local Tax Liabilities and Their Implications for Business Investment Location," *National Tax Journal* 39: 3 (September 1986): 357–66, and Leslie E. Papke, "Subnational Taxation and Capital Mobility: Estimates of Tax-Price Elasticities," *National Tax Journal* 40: 2 (June 1987): 191–203.

may constrain a booming economy in which private sector employers are having difficulty finding new hires.[10]

Tariffs and quotas can reduce imports and save jobs in industries competing directly with foreign competition. However, import restrictions limit consumer choice to higher-priced products—because of the reduced supply of competing foreign goods[11]—and, by protecting domestic industry, reward inefficiency and discourage productivity gains. Decreased productivity and increased prices reduce the growth of pay and its purchasing power, thereby lowering domestic living standards. Foreign countries' retaliatory tariffs and quotas compound these problems. In any event, the short-run protection of any specific industry does not address economy-wide unemployment.

Finally, work-sharing, shortening the work week in order to spread the available work among more employees, is not generally thought to be a viable employment policy. The costs associated with each individual employed, especially that of providing health insurance and other fringe benefits, spread over fewer work hours, effectively raise labor costs per hour. By increasing the cost of labor, work-sharing would motivate employers to cut their work forces, thus countering the direct effect of work-sharing.[12]

Although exogenous to the labor market, education, both within schools and thereafter, affects the skills applicants bring to employers and the set of jobs for which they can qualify. Policy options for skill acquisition range from educational vouchers for elementary and secondary schools to government-provided employment and training programs.

Government training programs have had modest beneficial effects on the employment and earnings of their participants, usually stronger for women than for men, and for minorities than for white Anglos. For example, the Comprehensive Employment and Training Act ("CETA") increased participants' postprogram annual earnings in the 1970s by $200 to $600. On-the-job training for which private sector employers were reimbursed and public sector employment were generally more effective than classroom training or work experience programs involving subsidized jobs with nonprofit or public employers.[13]

10. Alan Fechter, *Public Employment Programs* (Washington: American Enterprise Institute for Public Policy, 1975), and George E. Johnson, "Do We Know Enough about the Unemployment Problem to Know What, If Anything, Will Help?" pp. 37–57 in Bawden and Skidmore, eds., *Rethinking Employment Policy*, esp. pp. 41–47.

11. Also, domestic firms purchasing foreign machinery or other goods that will be components in their final products will face higher costs when tariffs and quotas are imposed. The prices of their final products will therefore increase.

12. See chap. 2, note 5, for references on this issue.

13. Burt S. Barnow, "The Impact of CETA Programs on Earnings: A Review of the Literature," *Journal of Human Resources* 22: 2 (Spring 1987): 157–93.

Because these programs can cost several thousand dollars per enrollee, participants' increased income of a few hundred dollars must be sustained for many years in order for programs to have favorable cost-benefit profiles. Most researchers have had the opportunity to analyze participants' earnings for only a few years.[14]

Among the most effective—and cheapest—training programs are those instructing enrollees in job-seeking skills, including clothing and grooming advice and interviewing techniques. Participants in CETA "Job Clubs" and "Job Factories" found work much faster than their peers not receiving counseling.[15]

7.2 Inner-City Unemployment

Many inner-city minority job seekers live in areas where the drug trade is flourishing and other employment opportunities are diminishing. Participation in illegal drug dealing is a substitute for legal employment that could provide skills, references, and work histories to stand minority applicants in good stead in competition for jobs. In particular, minorities convicted of drug possession or sale will be screened out during many employers' initial applicant evaluations.

Furthermore, employers' reluctance to locate in high crime areas inhibits the creation of jobs in the inner cities. And not only have some businesses relocated to the suburbs, but the total number of domestic manufacturing jobs has declined. Finally, declining demand for unskilled workers has several implications for minority workers within cities and elsewhere.

7.2.1 Drugs and Crime

The illegal status of drugs has serious consequences for the labor market for minority workers, particularly young black males: "Among blacks, one-fifth of 16–34 year old men and as many as three-fourths of 25–34 year old [male] high school dropouts had criminal records in the 1980s."[16] First, participation

14. Ibid. and Burt S. Barnow, "Government Training as a Means of Reducing Unemployment," chap. 5, pp. 109–35, in Bawden and Skidmore, eds., *Rethinking Employment Policy,* discuss the uncertainty in estimating these effects and difficulties arising from the use of some comparison groups. Initial results of a recent study of the U.S. Department of Labor's Job Training Partnership Act using a control group—to which interested job seekers were randomly assigned as an alternative to becoming program participants—indicates modest effects for adults, especially women, but no positive—and often negative—impact for out-of-school sixteen- to twenty-one-year-olds. See Abt Associates, "The National JTPA Study: Title II-A Impacts on Earnings and Employment at 18 Months, Executive Summary" (Bethesda, Md., 1992).

15. Robert G. Wegmann, "Job-Search Assistance: A Review" (University of Houston at Clear Lake City, 1979).

16. Richard B. Freeman, "Crime and the Employment of Disadvantaged Youths," chap. 6, pp. 201–37, in Peterson and Vroman, eds., *Urban Labor Markets and Job Opportunity.*

in illegal drug dealing involves crimes of possession and sale that, although not as threatening as the violent crimes ancillary to drug traffic, nonetheless lead to arrests and convictions that can drastically reduce legal job opportunities when employers summarily reject job seekers with criminal records. In particular, incarceration and probation have long-term adverse effects on the employment and income of young men.[17] If police are concentrated in inner-city neighborhoods or otherwise more likely to question minority citizens, minorities will be more likely than whites to be arrested for even minor infractions and to suffer the labor market consequences.[18]

Second, because the illegal drug trade is highly remunerative, particularly when compared with alternative opportunities for youngsters, it attracts those who would otherwise seek conventional jobs. The opportunity cost of selling drugs is the forgone acquisition of skills and experience in legal occupations that could have increased young people's future pay and employment. Job applicants with previous experience in drug dealing not only cannot compete for conventional jobs against peers with prior relevant experience, but they also present to employers work histories indicating little or no legal employment of any kind.[19]

Third, employers are less likely to locate in high crime areas because they fear theft and violence, are aware that potential customers and employees have the same fears, and realize that they would have to incur relatively high security and insurance costs. Because of the geographic correlation between areas of drug traffic and high minority unemployment, drugs particularly inhibit employment opportunities in minority neighborhoods.

7.2.2 Job Location

The spatial mismatch hypothesis states that the lack of jobs for inner-city residents is in part the product of an exodus of both people and firms from cities to suburbs. Both the decline in the number of manufacturing jobs and the suburbanization of employment are correlated with lower employment rates for blacks (as well as whites) in the cities than in the suburbs,[20] but not with metropolitan-area black unemployment.[21] Black and Hispanic male

17. Ibid., p. 201.

18. For further discussion of crime and race, see chap. 9, "Crime and the Administration of Criminal Justice," pp. 451–507, in Jaynes and Williams, *A Common Destiny.* Among their conclusions is (p. 471): "Middle-class and near-poor blacks seem to suffer significantly greater losses [from crime] than poor blacks or than whites of any income level."

19. These effects are attenuated for those whose drug trafficking is only moonlighting.

20. Harry J. Holzer and Wayne P. Vroman, "Mismatches and the Urban Labor Market," chap. 3, pp. 81–112, and James H. Johnson, Jr., and Melvin L. Oliver, "Structural Changes in the U.S. Economy and Black Male Joblessness: A Reassessment," chap. 4, pp. 113–47, in Peterson and Vroman, eds., *Urban Labor Markets and Job Opportunity.*

21. Holzer and Vroman, "Mismatches and the Urban Labor Market."

unemployment is highest relative to that of white males in metropolitan areas where suburbanization of jobs is most prominent.[22] Inner cities have fewer employment opportunities associated with businesses serving the more economically well-off individuals who have relocated to the suburbs.

From 1981 to 1991, the United States economy lost half a million manufacturing jobs while the total number of jobs increased by almost twenty million. As a result, the proportion of jobs in the manufacturing sector decreased from 22 to 18 percent. During the same decade, the economy also lost a quarter of a million mining jobs, and the proportion of jobs in the mining sector dropped from 1 percent to one-half of 1 percent. The fastest-growing sector was services, adding ten million jobs in the decade, with its representation among all jobs increasing from 30 to 34 percent.[23] The decline in manufacturing is associated with a modest but significant drop in black employment, particularly for high school dropouts.[24] Older black men with experience in manufacturing plants that have closed cannot provide fruitful networks for younger blacks seeking jobs in today's service industries.[25] The changing industrial structure combined with the growth in white female labor force participation has produced a "surplus of unskilled workers in a market requiring more skill than ever."[26]

Not only has the number of manufacturing jobs been decreasing,[27] but new plants now tend to locate in the suburbs to take advantage of cheap land, access to highways, and low crime rates; in addition, businesses shun urban locations to avoid buying land from several different owners, paying high demolition costs for old buildings, and arranging parking for employees and customers.[28] An open question is the extent to which suburbanization of em-

22. John E. Farley, "Disproportionate Black and Hispanic Unemployment in U.S. Metropolitan Areas: The Role of Racial Inequality, Segregation, and Discrimination in Male Joblessness," *American Journal of Economics and Sociology* 40: 2 (April 1987): 129–50.

23. The data are for January 1981 and January 1991 from U.S. Department of Labor, Bureau of Labor Statistics, *Employment and Earnings* 28: 2 (February 1981): table A-24, and 38: 2 (February 1991): table A-25. Employment levels would be slightly but not markedly different for similar ten-year comparisons on other dates because of the varying reaction of sectors to changing economic conditions.

24. Holzer and Vroman, "Mismatches and the Urban Labor Market."

25. Jaynes and Williams, *A Common Destiny*, p. 321.

26. Gary Burtless, "Introduction and Summary," pp. 1–30, in Gary Burtless, ed., *A Future of Lousy Jobs? The Changing Structure of U.S. Wages* (Washington: Brookings Institution, 1990), p. 30.

27. See Barry Bluestone and Bennett Harrison, *The Deindustrialization of America: Plant Closings, Community Abandonment, and the Dismantling of Basic Industry* (New York: Basic Books, 1982), esp. chap. 2.

28. David T. Ellwood, "The Spatial Mismatch Hypothesis," pp. 147–85 in Freeman and Holzer, eds., *The Black Youth Employment Crisis*, p. 155.

ployment reflects firms' avoidance of areas with relatively many minorities (see section 6.3).

A summary of empirical studies concludes that job access—variously defined as the ratio of jobs to people within neighborhoods, or travel times from residences to jobs—has significant effects of uncertain magnitude on black youth employment both within and between metropolitan areas.[29] Studies not supporting the spatial mismatch hypothesis have been criticized on technical grounds, including the use of flawed spatial mismatch indicators.[30] In a program that can be viewed as a rare social experiment amenable to economic analysis, black families who moved from Chicago public housing to private housing in the suburbs experienced significantly higher employment rates than did their counterparts who moved to private housing within the city. New suburban residents explained this pattern by noting their decreased likelihood of being assaulted and increased comfort in letting their children be alone—as well as their expanded job opportunities.[31]

On the other hand, that "race, not space" matters is the conclusion of another Chicago study in which young blacks living on the West Side, an area with many employers, had no greater employment rates than those on the South Side, a neighborhood with few employers.[32] That is, "black and white teenagers living in the same neighborhoods fared just as differently as blacks and whites who live across town from each other."[33] Indeed, "Most teenagers, black and white, don't work in their neighborhoods. And in black areas where there are many jobs for youth, white youngsters tend to fill them."[34] This conclusion, which has been criticized on grounds that the West Side and South Side labor markets were similar, with the former having large establishments in rapid decline,[35] is of course consistent with the discussion of section 3.2 emphasizing intraethnic job networks and a low rate of black entrepreneurship.

That both race and space matter seems a safe conclusion. Additionally, the geographical dispersion of suburban jobs renders public transportation

29. See Harry J. Holzer, "The Spatial Mismatch Hypothesis: What Has the Evidence Shown?" *Urban Studies* 28: 1 (February 1991): 105–22, a summary of twenty years of empirical research.

30. John F. Kain, "The Spatial Mismatch Hypothesis: Three Decades Later," *Housing Policy Debate* 3: 2 (1992): 371–460.

31. James E. Rosenbaum and Susan J. Popkin, "Employment and Earnings of Low-Income Blacks Who Move to Middle Class Suburbs," pp. 342–56 in Jencks and Peterson, eds., *The Urban Underclass.*

32. Ellwood, "The Spatial Mismatch Hypothesis."

33. Ibid., p. 149.

34. Ibid.

35. John Kasarda, "Urban Industrial Transition and the Underclass," *Annals of the American Academy of Political and Social Science* 501 (January 1989): 26–47, esp. pp. 38–39.

impractical for many employees. Inner-city workers are employed in greater numbers in areas with bus service than in areas equally distant but without public transportation. Blacks are much less likely to own vehicles than are whites with similar characteristics—in part because black urban dwellers face particularly high costs of maintaining, operating, and insuring automobiles, especially in the older, larger, densely populated cities.[36]

In response to the employment-inhibiting black residential patterns, some have emphasized attacking housing discrimination, while others have proposed economic development of inner cities. In addition to the policies outlined in section 7.1, analysts have recommended job information systems matching city workers and suburban employers, restructured transportation systems, day care facilities and subsidies, and more protection for inner-city residents from violent criminals.[37]

7.2.3 The Market for Low-Skilled Labor

Less skilled workers, usually defined as those working in operative, laborer, and service occupations, or as high school dropouts, have fared very poorly in the last two decades. These workers are disproportionately minority (see table 6.4).

The changing industrial composition of the economy—from manufacturing to service jobs—and restructuring within industries have reduced the pay and employment opportunities of the least skilled workers, while increasing the demand for skilled labor. Large cities, in particular, formerly dominated by production of goods, are now centers of information processing.[38] As a result, the pay of unskilled labor has not even kept pace with inflation, let alone with the pay of skilled workers.[39]

The primary cause of the declining market for unskilled labor appears to be the technical change that has increased the productivity of skilled labor and thereby induced substitution of skilled workers and capital for unskilled labor within firms.[40] Other causes include increased international competition, ef-

36. Kain, "The Spatial Mismatch Hypothesis," pp. 432–36.

37. Ibid., pp. 442–50.

38. Kasarda, "Urban Industrial Transition and the Underclass."

39. McKinley L. Blackburn, David E. Bloom, and Richard B. Freeman, "The Declining Economic Position of Less Skilled American Men," pp. 31–67 in Burtless, ed., *A Future of Lousy Jobs?* esp. table 1, p. 32, focusing on 1973, 1979, and 1987 earnings for white male full-time workers at least twenty-five years old. Analyzing this group obviates investigating employment discrimination and the labor market for youths who have not completed their schooling.

40. John Bound and George Johnson, "Changes in the Structure of Wages in the 1980s: An Evaluation of Alternative Explanations," *American Economic Review* 82: 3 (June 1992): 371–92, and Lawrence F. Katz and Kevin M. Murphy, "Changes in Relative Wages, 1963–87: Supply and Demand Factors," *Quarterly Journal of Economics* 107: 1 (February 1992): 35–78.

fectively expanding the supply of unskilled labor, and the shift in the industrial composition of employment that has reduced manufacturing and other blue-collar job opportunities.

Low pay for unskilled workers has discouraged men's labor force participation. Moreover, since 1972, black men have reduced their labor force participation rates relative to white men commanding the same pay, so the decrease in black male labor force participation induced by low pay for unskilled labor has been especially steep.[41] Young black men also have reservation wages, below which they will not accept employment offers, comparable to those of similarly situated young whites. But because the pay blacks can realistically receive is lower than that of whites—because of discrimination or unobserved skills that render the blacks less qualified than whites to whom they are apparently similar—maintaining these reservation wages significantly increases blacks' duration of unemployment.[42]

7.3 Recruitment and Certification

What policies besides those already discussed might mitigate the effects of minorities' generally less fruitful job-seeking networks and counter the disproportionate initial summary rejection minority applicants face? That is, can we augment recruitment channels for minorities, and provide certification for them as competent employees that will counter generally less impressive work histories, educational attainment, and references?

7.3.1 Minority Business Formation

Given the prevalence of intraethnic hiring, businesses started by minorities would be expected to increase minority employment dramatically. Minority entrepreneurs not only benefit intraethnic job seekers but also may enhance the political clout of their communities and facilitate the growth of minority suppliers. In particular, businesses within black neighborhoods may attract additional establishments, thereby providing still more legal employment opportunities as alternatives to crime and, by increasing the viability and safety of their communities, retaining residents who would otherwise move. All these effects enrich job-seeking networks within the community. Indeed, the black share of total business is positively correlated with relative black income across cities.[43]

41. Juhn, "Decline of Male Labor Force Participation," p. 114.

42. Harry J. Holzer, "Reservation Wages and Their Labor Market Effects for Black and White Male Youth," *Journal of Human Resources* 21: 2 (Spring 1986): 157–77.

43. Wayne J. Villemez and John S. Beggs, "Black Capitalism and Black Inequality: Some Sociological Considerations," *Social Forces* 63: 1 (September 1984): 117–44.

Certainly, reducing inner-city crime and providing tax incentives will encourage business formation, including firms founded by minorities. But how to encourage minority businesses in particular is another issue.

A common perception is that minorities lack the wealth to start businesses, and face credit market discrimination that makes it difficult for them to obtain start-up loans. Indeed, blacks appear to receive smaller loans than whites with similar equity capital investments and educational backgrounds.[44] However, a 1982 survey indicates that more than one-quarter of businesses began with no start-up capital, and more than one-third of ventures needed less than $5,000. Thus, about 60 percent of white, 70 percent of black, and 65 percent of Hispanic businesses were started with less than $5,000. Furthermore, within each group, more than half the businesses that required capital were financed without the owner(s) having to borrow.[45] And, among small businesses established between 1976 and 1982, only 32 percent of the white male and 25 percent of the black businesses used commercial bank loans.[46] Nevertheless, a nest egg to tide owners over before their businesses bloom may be a prerequisite for entrepreneurship, and thus a wealth constraint associated with business formation.

The entrepreneurial talent and energy evident in drug dealing and other generally frowned-on activities perhaps can be harnessed toward legitimate ends. In the wake of the 1992 South Central Los Angeles riot, gang members were considering washing cars, designing clothes, and selling soda. The infusion of funds from corporate donors and well-wishers provided start-up capital for these enterprises not generally available to budding entrepreneurs.[47]

Many of these businesses are most promising in urban areas with many potential customers. The employment problems of minorities located in rural areas, notably American Indians, are less tractable.[48] Retail establishments serving local communities are limited by the sparse population. Businesses based on natural resource harvesting or tourism may be more promising. Migration to high-employment population centers is always an option.

Interestingly, minority businesses covered by antidiscrimination laws might face especially stringent regulation if they recruit via word of mouth. Assume

44. Timothy Bates, "Commercial Bank Financing of White- and Black-Owned Small Business Startups," *Quarterly Review of Economics and Business* 31: 1 (Spring 1991): 64–80.

45. See Bruce D. Meyer, "Why Are There So Few Black Entrepreneurs?" (Cambridge, Mass.: National Bureau of Economic Research Working Paper No. 3537, 1990), table 12.

46. Bates, "Commercial Bank Financing," p. 64.

47. John R. Emshwiller, "Rival Street Gangs Discover Capitalism, the Legitimate Kind," *Wall Street Journal*, June 22, 1992, p. A1.

48. Only 26.3 percent of all Americans, but 45.4 percent of American Indians, lived in rural areas in 1980. U.S. Department of Commerce, Bureau of the Census, *1980 Census of Population, General Social and Economic Characteristics*, U.S. Summary, table 72.

a labor market is 80 percent white and 20 percent black. A white owner will have to hire seventeen consecutive white employees before reaching the equivalent of a two-standard-deviation shortfall of blacks. Yet a black owner will reach a two-standard-deviation shortfall of whites after only three black hires.

7.3.2 Short-Term Employment

A minority applicant strongly recommended to a white business owner by that owner's friend, relative, neighbor, business associate, or employee stands an excellent chance of being hired, not to mention being considered as a serious applicant, even if the minority applicant's other characteristics would be such as to trigger a summary rejection: The trusted recommendation carries such weight that it often can negate the lack of other references, unimpressive education credentials, and a spotty work history. Accordingly, although education policies and the like are relevant for helping minority children develop future labor market skills, acquiring even one solid reference can help workers now in the labor force to get on the right track.

One proposal to help minorities acquire such references is to take advantage of a set of available job opportunities that often are not filled because of inefficient information transfer. For example, imagine a professional named Ms. Jones preparing a report late into the night for delivery the following morning. Ms. Jones would like some clerical support and would prefer that someone else deliver the report to the security guard at the office building where the report is due. But because of the time of night, she cannot call on one of her coworkers or a temporary service for clerical support. Nor can she contact her firm's messenger or a courier service. Assuming Ms. Jones is working in even a moderately densely populated area, almost surely someone nearby is willing and able to perform the clerical and courier services she needs. But because it would take Ms. Jones so long to find these people, she opts instead to do the work herself.

Similar situations abound within households, particularly those pressed for time but with ample wealth to afford help. Assume Mr. Smith would prefer eating a leisurely breakfast or arriving at work early to clearing snow from his sidewalk. But because it is time-consuming to find someone willing and able to shovel the snow, Mr. Smith does the job himself.

In both of these cases, information about the job opportunity cannot be transmitted quickly to those willing and able to do it. The job opportunities will have disappeared before prospective applicants can be made aware of them.

If information could be transmitted more efficiently, a Pareto-superior result could obtain. Ms. Jones and Mr. Smith would pay for help and be better off than they would be if they performed the tasks themselves. The individuals helping them would receive extra income, and, if they performed well, possibly develop a contact who will use their services again or refer them to others.

Yet a medium for such informational exchange already exists: the interactive telephone. Today telephones are used by people to get bank account information, place and answer personal ads, express preferences on questions posed to them on television, and the like. Thus, if those seeking workers or jobs placed ads similar to personals, or, in the alternative, could review and respond to short-term job opportunities by phone, moonlighting job seekers could be matched with those like Ms. Jones and Mr. Smith.

It should be relatively easy for a group of public-spirited citizens to establish such a telephone network. In the future, when computers become as ubiquitous as telephones now are, even more detailed information exchange will be possible. Some of the difficulties in implementing this scheme would soon become apparent. Two of the biggest problems for the short-term employers are having confidence that the recruited workers will be sufficiently competent and monitoring workers' performance. These issues vary considerably in importance: They are much more crucial for Ms. Jones working under a tight deadline than for Mr. Smith, who need not even meet the referred worker and, if worse comes to worst, can shovel his own sidewalk hours later.

A charitable organization might prescreen short-term workers, certify that some of them have performed adequately in previous assignments, or be liable if their referrals do not perform well. In this sense, the organization will provide something akin to a brand name for their referred workers that, as with retail products, suggests reliability or quality over and above that of a comparable generic product. Perhaps several competent assignments through this network will lead to referrals to long-run job opportunities. If nothing else, these opportunities can provide a secondary income source.

I would not expect these networks to increase minority employment dramatically. But I believe the idea is worth trying, and that its implementation may suggest other means by which job seekers and jobs can be matched.

7.3.3 Expectations

No matter what discrimination and employment policies are implemented, attitudes of individual employers and job seekers can substantially affect minority employment prospects. If employers were indifferent to job applicants' race and ethnicity, and had no preconceptions about ethnic productivity, the statistical discrimination discussed in section 3.1 would vanish. At the same time, if minority job seekers' direct or indirect experiences with employer discrimination were not generalized to all white employers, they would approach job seeking with an energy and enthusiasm that would increase their employment possibilities. Some observers would also stress the importance of cultural values that, holding constant economic conditions, will affect the extent to which youngsters in particular are drawn to legal jobs rather than illegal activities or dependence on government programs.[49]

A reduction in racial and ethnic social segregation would allow the fruitful word-of-mouth networks of whites and Asians to benefit blacks, Hispanics, and American Indians. In particular, without sharing these networks, increased housing integration may solve only part of the problems minority job seekers face.

Whatever people's attitudes or the extent of segregation, minority job seekers will be well served by focusing directly on improving their job-seeking networks, and by prospective employers' evaluating applicants' competence on the basis of what they can do now rather than by what they haven't done in the past.

49. See, for example, Lawrence Harrison, *Who Prospers? How Cultural Values Shape Economic and Political Success* (New York: Basic Books, 1992), John D. Kasarda, "Why Asians Can Prosper Where Blacks Fail," *Wall Street Journal,* May 28, 1992, p. A20, and James Q. Wilson, "How to Teach Better Values in Inner Cities," *Wall Street Journal,* May 18, 1992, p. A10.

AUTHOR INDEX

Abernathy, Ralph David, 111
Aigner, Dennis J., 30, 31
Arrow, Kenneth J., 80
Ashenfelter, Orley, 21, 90

Ballen, John, 21
Barnow, Burt S., 121–22
Barron, John M., 12, 22, 23, 24
Bates, Timothy, 44, 128
Beals, Ralph E., 53
Becker, Gary S., 29, 59, 79
Beggs, John S., 127
Belous, Richard S., 18
Bendick, Mark, Jr., 27
Best, Fred, 8
Bishop, John, 12, 22, 23, 24
Black, Dan A., 23, 24
Blackburn, McKinley L., 126
Bloch, Farrell E., 53, 75, 80
Bloom, David E., 126
Bluestone, Barry, 124
Borjas, George J., 30
Bound, John, 43, 91, 126
Braddock, Jomills Henry, II, 27, 35
Bradshaw, Thomas F., 26
Brimmer, Andrew F., 45
Brown, Charles, 24, 75, 78, 99
Burtless, Gary, 120, 124
Butler, Richard, 92, 98

Cain, Glen G., 30, 31, 79
Card, David, 93
Carter, Stephen, 84
Coase, Ronald H., 17

Corcoran, Mary, 26, 47
Cross, Harry, 34
Culp, Jerome McCristal, 35, 47, 95

Daniels, Roger, 77
Datcher, Linda, 13, 26
Denton, Nancy A., 35, 38
Dershowitz, Alan M., 46
Donohue, John J., III, 90, 91, 94, 100, 104, 112
Drucker, Peter, 19
Duncan, Greg J., 26
Dunham, Constance R., 44
Dunkelberg, William C., 12, 22, 23, 24
Dunson, Bruce H., 35, 47

Egan, Mary Lou, 27
Ehrenberg, Ronald G., 8
Eisner, Robert, 120
Ellwood, David T., 47, 124, 125
Emshwiller, John R., 128
Epstein, Richard A., 34, 75, 89, 95, 96

Farley, John E., 124
Fay, Robert, 58
Fechter, Alan, 121
Fix, Michael, 33, 34
Freeman, Richard B., 21, 43, 91, 118, 122, 123, 126
Friedman, Milton, 119

Gaines-Carter, Patrice, 32
Garrow, David J., 111
Genesove, David, 21

Gilroy, Curtis, 75
Goldberg, Matthew S., 30
Gottfredson, Linda S., 46
Granovetter, Mark S., 11, 15, 27
Gray, Wayne, 45
Griffin, Peter, 98
Grossman, Paul, 48, 51

Hamermesh, Daniel S., 24
Hamilton, James, 24, 78, 99
Harrison, Bennett, 124
Harrison, Lawrence, 131
Haveman, Robert, 119
Heckman, James J., 77, 90, 91, 92, 93, 94, 95, 98, 119
Hilaski, Harvey J., 25
Hoffman, Joan, 95
Holzer, Harry J., 24, 26, 123, 124, 125, 127
Horowitz, Donald L., 59

Jacoway, Elizabeth, 90
Jaynes, Gerald David, 47, 123, 124
Johnson, George E., 121, 126
Johnson, James H., Jr., 123
Juhn, Chinhui, 101, 127

Kain, John F., 125, 126
Kasarda, John D., 125, 126, 131
Katz, Lawrence F., 24, 126
Kenney, Genevieve, 34
Killingsworth, Mark R., 119
Kirschenman, Joleen, 35
Kirzner, Israel, 81
Kitano, Harry H. L., 77
Kohen, Andrew, 75
Krueger, Alan B., 24, 93

Lang, Kevin, 33
Lawson, Steven F., 90
Lees, Hannah, 111
Leonard, Jonathan S., 93, 96, 97, 98, 99
Lieberwitz, Risa L., 48
Loewenstein, Mark A., 23, 24
Lohr, Steve, 19
Loury, Glen C., 86
Lundberg, Shelly J., 30

Martinez, Tomás, 6, 15, 16, 18
Massey, Douglas S., 35, 38
McIntyre, Shelby J., 36

McPartland, James M., 27, 35
Medoff, James L., 24, 78, 99
Mell, Jane, 34
Meyer, Bruce D., 128
Mincy, Ronald B., 101
Moberg, Dennis J., 36
Morris, Aldon D., 111
Moss, Philip, 99
Murphy, Kevin M., 126

Neckerman, Kathryn M., 35
Newman, Jerry M., 36
Nozick, Robert, 74

Okun, Arthur M., 75
Oliver, Melvin L., 123

Palmer, John L., 119
Papke, James A., 120
Papke, Leslie E., 120
Pasel, Jeffrey, 58
Payner, Brook S., 77, 94, 95
Pencavel, John, 119
Peterson, George E., 35
Phelps, Edmund S., 6, 30
Player, Mack A., 48
Popkin, Susan J., 125
Posner, Barry Z., 36
Posner, Richard A., 106, 112n69

Rawls, John, 74
Rees, Albert, 13, 15, 26, 45
Riach, Peter A., 36
Rich, Judith, 36
Ricketts, Erol R., 101
Robinson, Gregory, 58
Rosenbaum, James E., 125
Rosenblum, Marc, 70
Rosenfeld, Carl, 26

Schlei, Barbara Lindemann, 48, 51
Schumann, Paul L., 8
Schwab, Stewart, 30
Sharf, James C., 46
Shoben, Elaine W., 48
Shultz, George P., 13, 15, 26
Siegel, Sidney, 53
Siegelman, Peter, 91, 100, 104
Smith, Adam, 23
Smith, James P., 43, 79, 108–9

Smith, Sharon P., 80
Sowell, Thomas, 71
Startz, Richard, 30
Stevens, David W., 25
Struyk, Raymond J., 33, 34

Tannen, Deborah, 33
Terrell, Henry S., 45
Thomas, Paulette, 33, 47
Tilly, Chris, 99
Turner, Margery Austin, 34

Villemez, Wayne J., 127
Vroman, Wayne P., 35, 123, 124

Waldinger, Roger, 44
Wegmann, Robert G., 122
Weiss, Andrew, 7
Welch, Finis R., 43, 79, 107, 108–9
Williams, Robin M., Jr., 47, 123, 124
Wilson, James Q., 131
Wilson, William Julius, 101
Woodward, C. Vann, 89

Zimmerman, Wendy, 34

SUBJECT INDEX

Administrative costs of regulation, 74, 86–87, 98, 116

Affirmative action: arguments for, 75, 76, 78, 79, 85–86; definitions, 70–71; externalities of, 84, 114, 116

Age discrimination, 29, 31, 38, 47, 48, 52, 54; and availability data, 3, 59–60

Age Discrimination in Employment Act, 52

Applicants: chilling of, 39; definitions, 6–7, 54; evaluation of, 6, 22–24, 54; in litigation, 1, 53–55, 60–61, 104; screening of, 6, 7, 8, 20–24, 109, 117; screening of minority, 1, 2, 28, 45–47, 118

Availability: age, 3, 59–60; definition, 3, 48, 52; determination, 56–60; in *EEOC v. O&G,* 66, 67–68; OFCCP requirements, 3, 52, 71–73, 112; sex, 58–59

Boycotts, 110–11

Business formation: and crime, 2, 101, 123, 126, 128; and minority employment, 4, 127–29. *See also* Entrepreneurship

Business necessity, 3, 49–50, 53, 64–65, 70, 113; in *EEOC v. O&G,* 68–69

Business services firms, 2, 8, 17, 18, 19–20

Castaneda v. Partida, 62 n24

Census Bureau, 55, 57

Census data, 40 n25, 44, 55, 109, 128 n48; in availability determination, 56–60; in *EEOC v. O&G,* 66, 67; undercount, 58

Civil Rights Act of 1866, Section 1981, 52

Civil Rights Act of 1871, Section 1983, 52

Civil Rights Act of 1964, 48–51, 52, 65, 111; coverage, 4, 49, 52, 78, 88, 100, 106; employment effects of, 1, 4, 45, 81, 88, 89–96, 103, 108–9, 117; public accommodations provisions, 45, 112

Civil Rights Act of 1990, 73

Civil Rights Act of 1991, 49–50, 64, 70, 73

Classified advertisements, 2, 6, 8, 14; job seekers' use of, 25–27; publications, 2, 3, 14, 37, 38, 45, 46, 50, 64, 110

Commerce, U.S. Department of, 55

Commuting distance: and availability, 58, 67; and hiring, 8, 10, 14, 22, 39, 46, 65, 68, 126; and pay, 2, 11, 13, 14, 39

Constitution, U.S., Article XXIV, 90

Crime: and applicant histories, 8, 21; and business formation, 2, 101, 123, 126, 128; and minority employment, 4, 47, 101, 109, 123

Cultural values, 44, 130–31; Asian, 77

Damages in litigation, 1, 104–5

Discrimination paradigm: common, 29–30; in economics, 4, 29 n1, 79–81

Disparate impact: defined, 50; and disparate treatment, 51, 53, 78–79; in *Griggs,* 50–51, 91; and recruitment practices, 53, 54, 110; and tests, 51, 83

Disparate treatment: and Civil Rights Acts of 1866 and 1871, 52; defined, 50; and disparate impact, 51, 53, 78–79; in *EEOC v. O&G,* 69

Drug traffic: and business formation, 2, 123;

and minority employment, 4, 101–3, 109, 122–23

Education, 121; and blacks' earnings, 93–94
EEO-1 reports, firms filing: in *EEOC v. O&G,* 66; race and sex composition of, 99, 105–9; regulation of, 86, 103, 115
EEOC, 94, 105, 113; budget and staffing, 91, 112; powers of, 49, 86
EEOC v. Chicago Miniature Lamp Works, 69nn41, 42
EEOC v. Consolidated Service Systems, 69n42
EEOC v. O&G Spring and Wire Forms Specialty Company, 3, 65–70, 94
Efficiency, 3, 74, 75, 79, 81–84, 87
Employment: black male, 43, 117–18; black-white, 43, 90–91; in enterprise zones, 120; race and sex, by sector, 1, 93, 105–9; short-term, 4, 129–30. *See also* Unemployment
Employment agencies, 2, 6, 8, 15–16, 17, 49; in ancient Sumer, 15, 18n18
Entrepreneurship: Asian, 77; black, 86, 125, 128; ethnic group and unemployment, 1, 3, 39–40, 43–45, 81, 109–10; minority, 4, 81, 127–29
Equal Employment Opportunity Act of 1972, 49, 51, 78, 88
Equal Pay Act of 1963, 52–53
Equity, 3, 74, 75, 79, 82, 85–86, 87
Executive Orders, 51–52, 70, 71
Externalities: of affirmative action, 84, 114, 116; of antidiscrimination regulation, 82, 83–84, 113–14, 116

Fair Labor Standards Act of 1938, 8, 53
Federal contract compliance program: availability methodology required, 3, 52, 71–73, 112; costs, 98, 112, 116; coverage, 84, 98; employment effects of, 1, 4, 88–89, 94, 96–99, 117; OFCCP budget and staffing, 97–98, 112; OFCCP regulation, 3, 48, 51–52, 70–73, 78, 103, 105, 112
Fringe benefits, 17, 31, 57, 85n22, 121; and size of employer, 24, 99; and temporary help agencies, 17, 18

Government employment, 65, 76, 110; as last resort, 120–21; regulation of, 49, 52
Griggs v. Duke Power Co., 50–51, 64, 91

Hazelwood School District v. United States, 62n24
Hiring discrimination, 29–36; and statistical discrimination, 30–33, 35; and statistical evidence, 53–64

Immigration Reform and Control Act of 1986, 34

James v. Stockham Valves and Fittings Company, 64
Jim Crow: and black employment, 89–90; repeal of, 94, 103, 111–12, 117; and South Carolina textile industry, 95–96. *See also* Segregation
Job location, 123–26; and employer avoidance of regulation, 4, 105–6, 124–25. *See also* Commuting distance
Job-seeking behavior, 6, 14–15, 110; methods used, 8, 25–27
Justice, U.S. Department of, 49

Labor, demand for, by skill, 1–2, 101, 109, 126–27
Labor force: definition, 43, 55, 117n1; participation, 43, 44, 58; participation and pay, 101, 119, 127
Labor, U.S. Department of: Bureau of Labor Statistics data, 25–26, 55, 124; Employment Service, 15; Employment and Training Administration, 15. *See also* Federal contract compliance program

Manufacturing, job losses in, 1, 101, 109, 123–24
Migration of blacks: regional, 94; suburban, 101
Minimum wage, 75, 118
Mister v. Illinois Gulf Railroad, 65n31
Monopoly and concentrated industries, 76–77
Monopsony, 95; and oligopsony, 77

Newark Branch N.A.A.C.P. v. Town of Harrison, N. J., 65n30

Occupational advancement: in EEO-1 filing firms, 93, 99, 108–9; among federal contractors, 98–99
Occupational licensing, 118–19
Overtime, 2, 8, 105, 115

Pareto-superiority, 82, 83, 111, 129

Pay, 2, 57, 93; black-white, 79, 80, 90–91, 93, 99; and commuting distance, 2, 11, 13, 14, 39; and damages, 104–5; male-female, 29, 79, 80; and word-of-mouth recruitment, 2, 8, 11

Productivity: and coworkers, 2, 10, 11, 28, 39, 68; and recruitment regulation, 82, 115; and word-of-mouth recruitment, 2, 8, 9–10, 11, 13, 68, 115

Recordkeeping requirements, 66, 86; and applicant definition, 7

Recruitment discrimination, 6, 28, 36–45, 51, 53, 60–61; in *EEOC v. O&G,* 65, 68–69

References, 10, 21–22, 47, 130

Regulation: alternatives to present, 113–16; avoidance by employers, 1, 4, 104–6, 114, 115–16, 124–25

Segregation, 29, 78; effects of repeal of, in South, 1, 4, 45, 94, 103, 109, 111–12, 117

Sex discrimination, 29, 31, 36, 47; and availability data, 58–59; and pay, 29, 79, 80; and unemployment, 40, 79–80

Size of employer: and applicant evaluation, 23–24; Census data on, 67; coverage by, under law, 4, 49, 88, 103–4; coverage by, under regulation, theoretical arguments, 3, 78, 79, 113, 114–16; and job stability, 24; and minority employment, 1, 88; and pay, 24, 99; and regulation avoidance, 105, 106; and statistical discrimination, 31; and use of business services, 20

Statistical discrimination, 28, 30–31, 32–33, 35, 47, 83, 130; and discrimination paradigm, 79–81; in *EEOC v. O&G,* 68

Statistical evidence, 3, 7, 48, 50, 53–64; in *EEOC v. O&G,* 66–68; and statistical significance, 50, 61–63, 105, 114

Stereotypes, 2, 34–35, 95, 100, 130

Targeted recruitment, 2, 8, 16–17, 71, 105, 109; and recruitment discrimination, 37–39, 45, 51, 53, 64, 67, 68

Tariffs and quotas, 121

Taxation: and business location, 105; and IRS regulation, 86–87; and public policy, 118, 119–20

Temporary help agencies, 2, 8, 17, 18–19, 114

Terry Properties, Inc. v. Standard Oil Company, 106 n59

Testers: phone inquiries, 32; walk-ins, 33–34; written submissions, 35–36

Tests, employment, 2, 6, 22, 31, 46 n35; and disparate impact, 51, 54, 64, 83

Textile industry: and monopsony, 77, 95; in South Carolina, 94–96

Training, 16, 121–22

Transfer programs, 93, 119

Turnover: and applicant evaluation, 23; and black employment gains, 95; and commuting distance, 14, 22, 39, 46; and coworkers, 2, 12; defined, 10; in discrimination paradigm, 80; and word-of-mouth recruitment, 2, 8, 12, 13

Unemployment: and applicant histories, 8, 21, 46–47; black-white, 1, 4, 40–43, 109; and damages, 104; and drugs and crime, 122–23; ethnic group, 16, 58, 77, 79–80, 81, 100, 113, 116; ethnic group and entrepreneurship, 1, 3, 39–40, 43–45, 81, 109–10; inflation trade-off, 6; and job location, 123–26; male-female, 40, 79–80; public policy, 117–22, 126, 129–30; and skill, 40, 126–27

Unemployment insurance, 16, 54

Unions, 39, 49, 75 n4, 85 n22, 93; hiring halls of, 15, 118 n3

Voting Rights Act of 1965, 90

Walk-ins, 2, 8, 14–15; in *EEOC v. O&G,* 68, 69; job seekers as, 25–27; and size of employer, 24

Wards Cove Packing Co. v. Atonio, 3, 49–50, 65, 69

Watson v. Fort Worth Bank & Trust, 49 n6

Word-of-mouth recruitment, 7–8, 9–13; and business necessity, 64, 68, 69, 113; and complexity of jobs, 10, 11; job seekers' use of, 25–27; and minority employment, 1, 3, 45, 46, 70, 81, 83, 86, 88, 101, 103, 109–10, 125, 131; and pay, 2, 8, 11; and productivity, 2, 8, 9–10, 11, 13, 68, 115; and recruitment discrimination, 28, 38, 50, 51, 53, 65, 82, 113; and size of employer, 2, 10–11, 12, 13, 24, 39, 88, 110; and turnover, 2, 8, 12, 13

Work-sharing, 8, 121